PANZER IV
vs
CHAR B1 BIS
France 1940

STEVEN J. ZALOGA

First published in Great Britain in 2011 by Osprey Publishing,
PO Box 883, Oxford, OX1 9PL, UK
PO Box 3985, New York, NY 10185-3985, USA
Email: info@ospreypublishing.com

Osprey Publishing, part of Bloomsbury Publishing Plc.

Transferred to digital print on demand 2014.

First published 2011
3rd impression 2012

Printed and bound by
Cadmus Communications, USA.

A CIP catalogue record for this book is available from the
British Library.

Print ISBN: 978 1 84908 378 2
PDF e-book ISBN: 978 1 84908 379 9

Page layout by Ken Vail Graphic Design, Cambridge, UK
Index by Alison Worthington
Typeset in ITC Conduit and Adobe Garamond
Maps by Bounford.com
Originated by PDQ Digital Media Solutions, Suffolk, UK

The Woodland Trust
Osprey Publishing are supporting the Woodland Trust, the
UK's leading woodland conservation charity, by funding the
dedication of trees.

www.ospreypublishing.com

Author's note

I would especially like to thank David Lehmann and Dr. Dirk
Rottgardt for their extensive help with research material used
in this book. Thanks also go to the late Col. Aubry, founder of
the Musée des Blindés at the French cavalry school at
Saumur, who was most helpful on my visits there back in
the early 1990s.

Glossary

ABS	Ateliers de Bourges (Bourges Arsenal)
BCC	Batalion des Chars de Combat (Tank Battalion)
BCG	Batallion des Chars de la Gendarmerie (Tank Battalion of the State Police)
BW	Battalionführerwagen (battalion commander's vehicle)
DCr	Division Cuirasée (Armored Division)
DI	Division d'Infanterie (Infantry Division)
DIM	Division d'Infanterie Motorisée (Motorized Infantry Division)
DLM	Division Légère Méchanique (Light Mechanized Division)
FCM	Forges et Chantiers de la Méditerranée (Mediterranean Forge and Shipyard)
FOV	field-of-view
GRDI	Groupe de reconnaissance d'Infanterie (Infantry Reconnaissance Group)
IRGD	Infanterie-Regiment Großdeutschland
Pz.Rgt.	Panzer Regiment
PzKpfw	Panzerkampfwagen (tank)
RCC	Régiment de Chars de Combat (Tank Regiment)
RI	Régiment d'Infanterie
TRC	tracteurs de ravitaillement chenillés (tracked supply vehicle)
ZW	Zugführerwagen (platoon commander's vehicle)

CONTENTS

INTRODUCTION

The Battle of France in May–June 1940 was the first military campaign to see large-scale tank-vs.-tank fighting. Only a handful of tank-vs.-tank clashes had occurred in World War I, and they were rare during both the Spanish Civil War and the Poland campaign of 1939 as well. The Battle of France was also the first campaign to see the use of armored divisions by both sides. This book examines the clashes between two of the best tanks of the 1940 French campaign, the French Char B1 bis and the German PzKpfw IV.

Tanks had emerged from World War I as an important, but flawed, innovation. Advances in firepower such as the machine gun and long-range artillery were better used as defensive weapons and led to the stagnation and horrors of trench warfare in 1914–18. The early tanks were a reincarnation of medieval siege engines, fragile but powerful weapons capable of cracking open a fortified trench line. The big question in the interwar years was whether tanks could help restore the battlefield balance by challenging the murderous firepower of the defense with enough mobility and armored protection to sustain offensive missions. The answer was by no means clear because early tanks were not durable enough to conduct operations for much more than a day or two before breaking down, becoming trapped in trenches, or exhausting their fuel supply. Tank technology improved in the 1920s and early 1930s, but the French Army remained saddled with its rusting Great War tanks. Their dismal automotive performance poisoned the attitudes of many French commanders to the potential of tanks beyond their limited role as infantry support weapons.

In Germany, the Kaiser's army had been unenthusiastic about tanks in World War I and had the smallest armored force of the Great Powers. The Versailles treaty banned tanks from the postwar Reichswehr but the ban had perverse consequences. Germany was not burdened with archaic tanks that might discourage army interest in mechanization. By explicitly banning tanks, the Allies merely convinced the Germans that the forbidden must be very desirable. Even relatively conservative German officers saw a necessity to acquire tanks as soon as possible to assuage this affront to the German Army's honor. Between the end of the war in 1918 and Hitler's rise to power in 1933, the German attitude towards tanks completely reversed, and the German Army began to emerge as an enthusiastic proponent of armored warfare.

Some far-sighted German officers saw the tank as more than a mere technical innovation, but as the seed for a revolution in warfare, shifting the balance back to the offensive in place of the defensive stagnation of World War I. The panzers were the steel core of a more elaborate effort at combined-arms mechanization and the panzer divisions included a balanced mix of tanks, mechanized infantry, and motorized artillery. The panzer divisions saw their vindication in Poland in September 1939, but it was one thing to defeat the outnumbered Poles and another thing to take on the vaunted French Army.

The French Army regarded the tank as a vital element in its doctrine of methodical battle. French doctrine was preoccupied with the lessons of World War I, convinced that the infantry needed a steel backbone of tank support to survive against the deadly firepower of the modern battlefield. The majority of French tanks were committed to the mission of infantry accompaniment. At the same time, the French recognized the need for mobile forces to carry out other missions. The tank offered a mechanized alternative to the horse for the traditional cavalry missions of reconnaissance and exploitation. As a result, the French devoted about a quarter of their tank force to this mission. These light mechanized divisions (DLM) were the closest French equivalent to the German panzer divisions, but they were far fewer in number in 1940: only three divisions compared to ten German panzer divisions. The French also saw the need for a heavily armored shock force to support the advance of the infantry, but

Like the Tiger tank later in the war, in 1940 the Char B1 bis was largely invulnerable to most enemy anti-tank weapons of the time. "Jeanne d'Arc" (no. 425) of the 1/47e BCC attacked a German bridgehead at Doudelainville, southwest of Abbeville, in the late afternoon of May 28, 1940. Under the command of Capt. Dirand, the tank destroyed two German 37mm anti-tank guns with its 75mm gun, but had that gun put out of action when a round struck inside the 75mm barrel. It continued its attack using its machine guns. Near Croisettes, it came under intense fire from numerous weapons of various calibers but the rounds bounced off its thick armor. It crushed several German guns under its tracks. It was finally hit on the left side by a heavy caliber gun, probably an 88mm, and put out of action. It received over 90 hits in two hours of fighting and destroyed about a dozen guns and two armored cars. (Patton Museum)

5

The PzKpfw IV was weakly armored and its firepower was inadequate against contemporary French tanks. However, it had a reliable and robust design that would become the workhorse of the Wehrmacht later in the war after being modernized and improved. This is a PzKpfw IV Ausf. D of Pz.Rgt.9, 10.Panzer Division on exercise in April 1940 at the Baumholder training grounds. (NARA)

there was no consensus until the German demonstration of panzer divisions in Poland in 1939. In early 1940, the French Army began consolidating their new Char B1 bis tank battalions into their own embryonic armored divisions (DCr). The French armored divisions were much smaller than their German counterparts and were not a well-balanced combined arms force. They were especially weak in motorized infantry. However, their main flaw was not organizational but chronological. They were created too late to undergo proper training; only two were fully organized by May 1940, and they lacked the practical experience of their German opponents.

The German Army in 1940 enjoyed significant tactical and organizational advantages over their French opponents, particularly in the areas of training and experience. However, the French Army held a slight edge in the number of tanks, and in many cases had better tanks. The Char B1 bis tank was the most powerful of its era. Not only was it armed with an impressive combination of both a 75mm gun and an excellent 47mm gun, but its thick armor was nearly impervious to German tank and anti-tank guns. The Char B1 bis' main weakness was an awkward design that can be traced back to its premature genesis in 1920. The PzKpfw IV was a robust and sound design, but like most German tanks of the era, it was weakly armored since the Wehrmacht favored speed and surprise over firepower and defense. It was designed to support the PzKpfw III main battle tank with high-explosive firepower, so its short 75mm gun was not effective in tank fighting. In spite of the technological imbalance in favor of the French, the German panzer units prevailed in most of the major tank engagements of the campaign.

The focus of this book is the combat duel at Stonne which pitted the PzKpfw IV tanks of Pz.Rgt.8, 10.Panzer Division against the two Char B1 bis battalions of the 3e DCr. The battle of Stonne was compared by one German officer to Stalingrad and Monte Cassino in its ferocity; it was grimly called the "Verdun of 1940" by German and French veterans alike.

CHRONOLOGY

January 1920 Development of Char B battle tank begins.

May 1924 Delivery of prototypes of Char B.

March 1929 Delivery of Renault prototype for Char B1.

1930 Begleitwagen prototypes completed by Rheinmetall-Borsig and Krupp.

April 1934 Production contract for Char B1.

1935 Development contract for engineering development of Begleitwagen awarded to Krupp.

Summer 1935 First panzer division begins formation at Munster.

December 1935 First Char B1 series-production tank delivered.

October 1936 Production contract for Char B1 bis.

February 1937 First Char B1 bis series-production tank delivered.

Autumn 1937 Production of Panzerkampfwagen IV begins.

1938

January First three PzKpfw IV Ausf. A issued to troops.

January 20 First Char B1 battalion declared operational.

April Production of PzKpfw IV Ausf. B begins.

May Production contract for 35 PzKpfw IV Ausf. A completed.

September Production contract for 42 PzKpfw IV Ausf. B completed; production of PzKpfw IV Ausf. C begins.

September 30 First Char B1 bis battalion declared operational.

1939

August Production contract for 134 PzKpfw IV Ausf. C completed.

September 1 Germany invades Poland starting World War II in Europe.

September French Army begins forming first Demi-brigade Lourde with Char B1 bis tanks.

October Production of PzKpfw IV Ausf. D begins.

1940

January French Army begins formation of first two Division Cuirasée.

May 10 Wehrmacht initiates Fall Gelb, the plan for the invasion of France.

May 13 Panzergruppe Kliest reaches the Meuse river and begins crossings.

May 14 French Army's first counterattack of Meuse bridgehead near Sedan by the 55e DI fails.

May 15 10.Panzer Division and the French XXI Corps begin battle for Stonne.

May 17 After two days of intense tank fighting around Stonne, both sides pull away their tank units for other missions and substitute infantry divisions.

June 21 Armistice signed ending the French campaign.

DESIGN AND DEVELOPMENT

THE CHAR B1 BIS

Although the Char B1 bis was the most powerful tank on the 1940 battlefield, in some respects it was among the more archaic. The awkward design of the Char B1 bis was due to the rapid evolution of tank technology and tank tactics during its two decades of gestation. In January 1920, the French war ministry set up a commission, under Gén. Buat, to determine the need for future tanks. The father of the French tank force in World War I, Gén. Jean-Baptiste Estienne, sought a new 15-ton tank design that would bridge the gap between the Renault FT light tank and the monstrous FCM 2C breakthrough tank. The tactical imperative for the *char de bataille*, or "battle tank," was that it would have enough armor to resist enemy field guns of the type encountered in the 1918 fighting; have the firepower to destroy typical defensive field works; have the mobility to surmount trenches and battlefield obstructions; and have the speed to penetrate enemy defenses. Estienne turned to a group of five French manufacturers for their concepts, and prototypes were delivered in May 1924. After trials lasting through March 1925, Estienne isolated the best features from each design, but strongly favored features of the Renault and FCM (Forges et Chantiers de la Méditerranée). It was at this stage that the Char B received its most dubious feature, a hull-mounted 75mm gun. It is unclear why the design called for this awkward addition considering that the Renault FT of 1917 had already proved the value of a turreted gun, and that FCM

had already designed two tanks, the Char 1A and Char 2C, with large-caliber guns in their turrets.

After tests, another round of prototypes were then ordered from Renault, FAMH (Forges et Aciéries de la Marine et d'Homécourt/St. Chamond) and FCM in March 1927. The first was delivered by Renault in March 1929 and early tests led to a decision to change the specifications on the remaining two pilots. These differed by requiring a 47mm gun in the turret instead of machine guns, and the armor basis was increased from 25mm to 40mm. What had started as a 13 metric ton tank had evolved into a 22-ton design with much more powerful armament.

One of the primary impediments in the development of the Char B was a lack of consensus over the tactical role of this tank. Although the Army retained a tank inspectorate after the 1918 armistice, it was subordinated to the infantry branch instead of the artillery branch which had been responsible for the *artillerie speciale* during the Great War. The infantry had a clear understanding of its requirements for an infantry accompanying tank, but the mission and technical characteristics for a battle tank remained unsettled. About the only area of design where there was a clear

The original production batch of Char B1 tanks served with the 511e RCC and, as seen here, were a popular spectacle on the Champs Elysées at the Bastille Day parades in Paris in 1938–39. Although the Char B1 tanks were retired prior to the France campaign, many were returned to service in ad-hoc companies in the spring of 1940, often rearmed with the 47mm SA 35 gun. This one, "Dunquerque" (no. 111), was attached to the 347e CACC and was destroyed during the fighting at Neuvy-sur-Loeilly on June 6, 1940. (NARA)

9

consensus was in the realm of armor protection. In contrast to the German preference for mobility at the expense of armor, the French Army clearly sought the best protection possible on its battle tank at the expense of mobility.

The Char B bore a certain resemblance to British Landships of the Great War with flat plate tracks running around the entire length and height of the hull. The main gun in the hull was a short 75mm weapon developed by Ateliers de Bourges (ABS) from the Mle. 31 fortress gun. It was primarily intended for attacking field works, bunkers and other targets because tank-vs.-tank fighting in World War I had been so rare; indeed there were no known instances of French tanks encountering German tanks in 1917–18. The 75mm gun was poorly suited to tank fighting due to its location and peculiar traverse system. Instead of using a dedicated gunner, the gun was traversed in azimuth using the sophisticated Naeder hydrostatic driving controls and aimed using a stereoscopic sight by the driver. While technically clever, this overly complicated configuration proved most unfortunate in actual service use.

The initial production was awarded for the Char B1 on April 6, 1934, and aside from the three prototypes, a total of 32 series-production tanks were built by Renault

CHAR B1 BIS "EURE" (NO. 337, CAPT. PIERRE BILLOTTE), 1E COMPAGNIE, 41E BCC, 3E DCR, MAY 1940.

Crew: 4	**Machine guns:** two co-axial 7.5mm Riebel MAC 31, 5,100 rounds
Length: 6.37m	
Width: 2.5m	**Engine:** Renault 307hp V-6
Height: 2.79m	**Fuel:** 400 liters
Combat weight: 31.5 metric tons	**Range:** 95–180km
Hull gun: 75mm SA 35 L/17, 74 rounds	**Top speed:** 28km/h
Turret gun: 47mm SA 35 L/32, 50 rounds	**Armor:** 60mm front, 60mm side, 55mm rear

EURE

337

6.37m

and FCM through April 1935, some 15 years after the design had begun. This differed from the German Pzkpfw IV where the archaic Großtraktor was abandoned for the more modern PzKpfw IV. However, the French Army had invested so much time and money in the Char B that it remained the focus of its battle tank program in spite of its many antiquated features. The archaic design was not rejected for a more modern configuration because of the lack of any strong doctrinal influence from the Army. In the German case, the advent of the panzer divisions provided a clearer direction for the technical features needed for a modern battle tank, while in the French case, the continuing lack of consensus about the need for armored divisions created a doctrinal vacuum that provided no clear directions to the tank industry.

The pre-series Char B built by Renault in 1929 still used a small machine gun turret, as seen here, shifting to a 47mm gun as the design was refined. (Patton Museum)

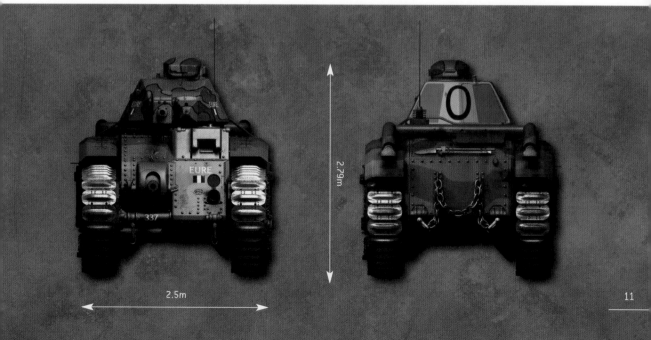

2.79m

2.5m

The definitive Char B1 bis was fitted with the APX-4 turret with the longer 47mm SA 35 gun. "Vertus" (no. 372) was delivered to the 41e BCC on November 29, 1940, and is seen here in the spring of 1940 during training. It was commanded by Lt. Jacques Hachet of 3/41e BCC and took part in the fighting at Stonne. After being separated from the battalion during the confused fighting, the tank suffered mechanical problems and was sent back to rear area repair base in early June 1940. (NARA)

The Char B1 series production was delivered from December 1935 through January 1937 to companies of the 2/511e RCC (2e Batalion, 511e Régiment de Chars de Combat) which were trained and combat ready by January 1938. In August 1939 this battalion was mobilized as the 37e BCC (Batalion des Chars de Combat). The original Char B1 design revealed numerous design defects and so rather than continue production, the upgraded Char B1 bis was developed. The main armor was increased from 40mm to 60mm and the turret armor was also increased to 60mm. The original APX1 turret with the short 47mm SA 34 gun was replaced by the APX4 turret with the longer 47mm SA 35, which was better suited to tank fighting. The heavier armor led to a redesign of the engine to increase power from 200 to 300 horsepower by adding a second carburetor, but this came at the expense of endurance which fell from eight hours to five hours between refueling.

An initial production order for 35 Char B1 bis tanks, enough to equip a single battalion, was signed in October 1936. This initial contract batch was delivered from February 1937 through March 1938 to the 1e/510e RCC in Nancy, which was mobilized in August 1939 as the 15e BCC. Starting in January 1939, the second contract batch went to the 1e/508e RCC in Luneville, which was mobilized as the 8e BCC in August 1939. The third batch went to the 2e/512e RCC in Châlons-sur-Marne in the summer of 1939, which was mobilized on August 28, 1939, as the 28e BCC. By the time of the war's outbreak on September 1, 1939, a total of 35 Char B1 and 84 Char B1 bis had been delivered and a total of 350 were on order. The next

units equipped were the 41e and 49e Battalions starting in January 1940 followed by the 37e Battalion which converted from the old Char B1 to the new Char B1 bis. By the time of the German attack on May 10, 1940, 258 Char B1 bis had been delivered to eight battalions. The tempo of production of the Char B1 bis increased from about seven per month in 1939 to about 32 per month in 1940 and by the end of the campaign, 1,178 Char B1 bis had been ordered and 403 completed by Renault, FCM, FAMH, AMX and Schneider.

The 75mm gun configuration was recognized as a problem during a series of firing trials, and the solution was to redesign the gun mounting to provide a limited amount of traverse for fine aiming. This was to be incorporated on the next version, the Char B1 ter, but this variant was only in prototype stage at the time the battle of France ended.

The high fuel consumption of the Char B1 bis prompted the deployment of the TRC 37L Lorraine which towed a special tracked fuel trailer. Six of these were deployed to support the ten Char B1 bis in each company, and contained enough fuel to refill all of the tanks. (NARA)

PANZERKAMPFWAGEN IV

Under the terms of the Versailles treaty that ended World War I, the Reichswehr was forbidden to have tanks. In spite of this, small-scale tank development was undertaken by means of a covert cooperative program with the Soviet Union. A joint training and experimental center was established at Kazan, where new German designs could be tested in secret. Tank development centered around two principal types, a Leichttraktor (light tractor) armed with a 37mm gun, and a Großtraktor (large tractor) armed with a short 75mm gun. The Großtraktor was the German analog of the Char B, though it had many differences. The 75mm main gun was mounted in a large turret rather than the hull. Although this proved to be much more satisfactory than the Char B's awkward arrangement, the Großtraktor had its share of anachronistic features. For example, a small machine gun turret was awkwardly positioned at the rear of the tank behind the turret, somewhat akin to the design of the French Char 2C breakthrough tank. In addition, the tank commander sat in the hull to the right of the driver, rather than in the turret. Experiments at Kazan from 1929 to 1933 with rival

OPPOSITE
The Großtraktor displayed
some similarity to the Char B1
in terms of general layout.
However, it mounted its main
75mm gun in the turret, and
a defensive machine gun in
a rear turret, which is not
evident in this view. One
of the key lessons from
experiments with this tank at
Kazan in Russia was that the
commander needed to be in
the turret, not in the hull as
he was with these tanks.
(Patton Museum)

versions of the Großtraktor, built by Krupp and Rheinmetall, helped the Reichswehr gain a better appreciation of contemporary tank design. The most important advantage of the Kazan program was that the Army made no commitment to serial production of the experimental tanks, and felt free to abandon these archaic designs when the re-militarization began after Hitler's accession to power in 1933.

In light of the Kazan experiments, the German Army's Motorization Department saw the need for two principal tank types, codenamed ZW and BW. The ZW (Zugführerwagen: section commander's vehicle) corresponded to the 37mm-armed Leichttraktor and was intended to be the principal battle tank. The BW (Battalionführerwagen: battalion commander's vehicle) corresponded to the 75mm-armed Großtraktor and was intended to be a fire-support tank to accompany the ZW. It would take several years before both new designs were ready, and German industry did not have the capability at the time to manufacture either type. As a result, a stop-gap light tank entered production as a means to equip the new panzer units and

PZKPFW IV AUSF. D, 7./PANZER REGIMENT.8, 10.PANZER DIVISION, MAY 1940

Crew: 5
Length: 5.92m
Width: 2.84m
Height: 2.68m
Combat weight: 20 metric tons
Main gun: 75mm KwK 37 L/24, 80 rounds
Elevation: −8 +20 degrees
Machine guns: one co-axial MG 34, one hull-mounted MG 34

Radio: FuG 5 transceiver
Engine: Maybach HL 120 TRM, 265hp
Fuel capacity: 470 liters
Range: 130–210km
Top speed: 42km/h
Armor: 35mm gun mantlet, 30mm front, 20mm side, 20mm rear

5.92m

to begin the process of mechanization. The Panzerkampfwagen I (PzKpfw. I) was later derided as a mere training tank, but the design was quite modern and efficient by early 1930s standards. It was armed with a pair of machine guns which had little capability for tank fighting, but it must be repeated that tank-vs.-tank fighting was extremely rare in World War I. One of its most important, if unheralded, attributes was good durability, about 1,800km between major overhauls compared to about 500km for contemporaries such as the Soviet T-26 tank. Continued delays in the ZW and BW tank programs, and the inadequate firepower of the PzKpfw I, forced the

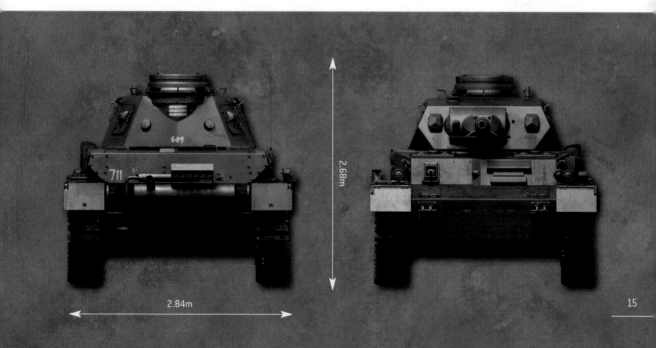

The PzKpfw IV Ausf. A was the original version of the series but only 35 were built. It differed from the later Ausf. D in many small ways and two of the more notable differences are the initial style of commander's cupola and the 75mm gun mount which lacked the mantlet shield. The doll in the Spanish uniform suggests that one of the crewmen may have been a Spanish Civil War veteran and served with the German detachment there. (NARA)

German Army to adopt another stop-gap tank in the mid-1930s, the PzKpwfw II armed with a 20mm automatic cannon. This tank was capable of fighting the lightly armored tanks common in Eastern Europe at the time such as the Polish 7TP or Soviet T-26, though it was less effective against French tanks, which were already moving towards heavier armor such as on the D1 infantry tank.

One of the most important tactical and technical lessons was the discovery, during the Kazan experiments, of the unsatisfactory crew layout of the Großtraktor. Placing the commander in the hull next to the driver was a significant mistake as he had a very poor view of the surroundings and found communication with the crew awkward because of his position. During the Kazan maneuvers, it was common for the commander to take over the loader's position in the Großtraktor turret, but this was tactically unacceptable for a number of reasons: it led to a reduction in the rate of fire during exercises; it made it difficult for the commander to spot enemy anti-tank guns; and it distracted the commander from staying in contact with other tanks in the unit. By 1932–33, a consensus had emerged that the commander should be moved up into the turret to his own station behind the gun, which would be fitted with a vision cupola that would permit hemispheric coverage. The Krupp three-man turret layout was accepted for both the ZW and BW designs. This helped establish the classic tank-turret layout for the next half-century. Soviet tanks of the 1930s relied on a two-man turret with the commander doubling up as the gunner or loader and French tanks were even worse with one-man turrets.

Development of a gun-armed ZW tank began in 1935, eventually entering production in 1937 as the PzKpfw III. This was the first medium tank in German production and was initially armed with a 37mm gun for commonality of ammunition with the new infantry anti-tank gun; Guderian pressed for a more powerful 50mm gun but was overruled. Use of the PzKpfw I in the Spanish Civil War from 1937 to 1939 made it clear that machine gun armed tanks were too vulnerable to gun-armed tanks such as the Soviet T-26, and this simply reinforced the existing consensus that a gun-armed tank like the PzKpfw III should form the backbone of the new panzer divisions. However, PzKpfw III production was very slow due to the need to address problems in its initial suspension, and only 98 were available at the start of the Poland campaign in September 1939.

The genesis of the PzKpfw IV was not due to concern over tank fighting, but rather to the need for a more powerful tank to assist in combating field works, and other enemy positions, with high-explosive firepower. It was armed with a short 75mm gun, dubbed the "cigar butt" by its crews. Development of the BW fire-support tank began in 1934 with three competing designs offered by Rheinmetall, MAN and Krupp. Krupp was awarded the engineering development contract in 1935 and production centered around the Krupp-Gruson plant in Magdeburg. Production of the initial PzKpfw IV Ausf. A started in October 1937 but only 35 were built before the improved Ausf. B was introduced in April 1938. Having learnt from chastening Spanish Civil War experiences, it was decided that this would have the frontal armor

The PzKpfw IV was armed with a short 75mm gun intended for fire support and not tank fighting. The Ausf. D variant, as seen here, had an added shield for the gun mantlet and returned to the use of a hull machine gun which had been deleted in the Ausf. B and C. This is a PzKpfw IV Ausf. D of 4./Pz.Rgt.1, 1.Panzer Division near Servance in June 1940. (NARA) thickened to 30mm, the engine and transmission improved, and a variety of other minor upgrades were included. It was followed in September 1938 by the PzKpfw IV Ausf. C which offered modest improvements over the Ausf. B. The next major evolutionary stage was the PzKpfw IV Ausf. D which was the definitive type at the time of the battle of France. This increased side armor from 15mm to 20mm and added an external mantlet to better protect the main gun opening on the turret front. The Ausf. D also reintroduced a hull machine gun which had been deleted on the Ausf. B and C. While the evolution of the PzKpfw IV saw a steady increase in armor, the German Army clearly favored mobility over armored protection. Indeed, the optimum level of armored protection on the PzKpfw IV at 30mm was essentially the starting point for French Char B armor which had steadily increased since 1921 from 30mm to 40mm and finally to 60mm.

By the outbreak of the war on September 1, 1939, there were 211 PzKpfw IV in service and 19 were lost during the Poland campaign; more than 50 required extensive overhauls due to battle damage or mechanical breakdown. The fighting in Poland

The PzKpfw IV commander had a vision cupola with five episcopes protected by armored visors. Unlike the Char B1 bis cupola, the German cupola had roof hatches to enable the commander to observe outside the tank, giving him better situation awareness, another useful practice that supported dynamic German panzer tactics. This is a PzKpfw IV Ausf. D of the 10.Panzer Division on exercise at the Baumholder training grounds in April 1940. (NARA)

showed the PzKpfw IV to be vulnerable to all modern anti-tank weapons including Polish anti-tank rifles and the Bofors 37mm anti-tank gun. This led to plans to increase the frontal armor to 50mm on the PzKpfw IV Ausf. E, but these did not become available until September 1940 after the France campaign. Production of the PzKpfw IV Ausf. D was stepped up after the Poland campaign, averaging 13 tanks monthly in 1939 but climbing to 20 tanks monthly in the first half of 1940. By May 1940, 290 PzKpfw IV were available for the France campaign. However, priority was clearly given to the PzKpfw III; production ramped up to over 50 monthly so that by May 1940, there were 381 available.

The PzKpfw IV's stablemate was the ZW tank, better known as the PzKpfw III. The PzKpfw III was intended to be the primary battle tank with the PzKpfw IV providing heavy fire support. This is a pair of PzKpfw III of 6./Pz.Rgt.9, 10.Panzer Division on exercise at the Baumholder training grounds in April 1940, shortly before the start of the France campaign. (NARA)

TECHNICAL SPECIFICATIONS

PROTECTION

The Char B1 bis offered superior armored protection to that offered by the PzKpfw IV. The Char B1 bis had 60mm armor on the front and sides, and 55mm of armor on the rear which made it essentially invulnerable to the 75mm gun of the PzKpfw IV. It was largely impervious to the German 37mm tank and anti-tank guns which

The Char B1 bis was well protected against German anti-tank guns but was not invulnerable to heavier caliber weapons. During the second week of June 1940, the 15 surviving tanks of the 41e BCC were split into three detachments and assigned various defensive tasks. Detachment Gasc, with three tanks, was assigned to protect Marne bridges. The major river crossing at Pogny-sur-Marne was defended by "Aisne" and "Beni-Snassen" which knocked out five German tanks on June 12, prompting the Germans to bring up 88mm or 105mm guns. This is "Aisne" (No. 339) of the 2/41e BCC which suffered two heavy caliber turret hits which killed the tank commander, Lt. Robert Homé. (NARA)

could penetrate 35mm of armor at 100 meters. About the only way to put a Char B1 bis out of action was to knock off the tracks, or to score a lucky hit on the engine grating on the left hull side.

The PzKpfw IV Ausf. D had 35mm armor on the gun mantlet, 30mm frontal armor and 20mm side and rear armor. This was inadequate at short ranges against the French 25mm infantry anti-tank gun which could penetrate 50mm of armor, and so it was even less effective against the French 47mm tank gun as used on the Char B1 bis or the more powerful 47mm towed anti-tank gun. The PzKpfw IV was especially vulnerable to catastrophic fires if the fighting compartment were penetrated. The right-side sponson contained ammunition stowage and the fuel tanks were located immediately below the turret basket. As will be noted in the Combat-Duel section below, of the five PzKpfw IV of Panzer Regiment.8 (Pz.Rgt.8) lost in the initial encounters at Stonne, two suffered catastrophic ammunition/fuel fires which blew the tanks apart.

FIREPOWER

The 75mm guns on both the Char B1 bis and PzKpfw IV were intended primarily for high-explosive firepower, and not for tank fighting. The 75mm SA 35 tank gun was relatively short with a caliber of L/17.1 and so had a relatively low initial muzzle velocity of 220m/s. It could penetrate the frontal armor of the PzKpfw IV at short ranges, but the main tank-fighting weapon used was the 47mm gun. The German KwK 37 "cigar butt" 75mm gun was slightly longer with a caliber of L/24, and so its projectile had a bit more speed with an initial muzzle velocity of 325m/s. Firing the

L.762 TELESCOPIC GUN-SIGHT, 47MM SA 35 GUN, CHAR B1 BIS (BELOW LEFT)

The commander's L.762 monocular telescopic sight operated at a single 4 power magnification and had an 11 degree FOV. The sight contained a pair of mechanically linked reticles consisting of a center aiming line with horizontal cross-hair, and a pair of range "stairs" on either side. The "stairs" on the left were for the MAC 31 machine gun (M = *mitrailleuse*) while the "stairs" on the right side had two separate gradations, the one on the left marked BR (R = *rupture*, armor-piercing) and the one on the right marked Ex (*explosif*, high-explosive). The commander rotated the reticle dial on the telescope to match the cross-hair with the appropriate range gradation, moving the cross-hair to provide the necessary super-elevation, and then the commander elevated the gun to align the re-aligned cross-hair with the point where he wished to aim. In the case seen here, the range reticle has been set to 200 meters on the BR "stair". As can be seen, the trajectory of the 47mm gun at this range is almost flat with very little compensation needed for ballistic fall.

L.710 TELESCOPIC SIGHT, 75MM SA 35 GUN, CHAR B1 BIS (ABOVE RIGHT)

The Char B1 bis employed a sophisticated stereoscopic range-finding binocular sight which was mechanically linked to the elevation gear. The sights provided a strong 4 power magnification with an 11 degree FOV. The reticle had only a single "stair" since the ballistic trajectory for both high-explosive and armor-piercing ammunition was essentially the same. When the driver focused the sight on the target, it provided a rough indication of range on the reticle which was used as the input for elevating the gun to compensate for the ballistic fall of the shot. In the case shown here representative of the view of Billotte's gunner, Sgt. Durupt, during the fighting in Stonne on May 16, the PzKpfw IV was encountered at very close range, essentially point-blank, where no super-elevation was needed.

TZF5B TELESCOPIC GUN-SIGHT, PZKPFW IV AUSF. D.

The 75mm KwK 37 gun on the PzKpfw IV was aimed using the Leitz TZF5b (Turmzielfernrohr) monocular telescopic gun-sight. This telescope operated at a single magnification of 2.5 power with a 25 degree FOV which was not especially strong for a tank telescope, but adequate for the type of missions envisioned for the tank. The sight contained two engraved reticles. The center reticle consisted of an aiming triangle in the center with smaller triangles on either side. The gunner placed the target at the apex of the center triangle. This reticle provided a limited stadiametric ranging capability which allowed a well-trained gunner to estimate the range based on the size of the target compared to the large triangle. The unit of measurement was a graduation (strich) equaling 1 meter at 1,000 meters range with the larger triangle having sides of 4 graduations and the smaller triangle having sides of 2 graduations. Such calculations were too difficult in the heat of battle, so a gunner had to be so well trained that the procedure became instinctive. In actual practice, the gunner's often used the co-axial machine gun to determine range. The series of triangles was intended to provide the gunner with a method to gauge the speed of a crossing target, but once again, this was too complicated to calculate during real engagements and depended on excellent training.

The second reticle provided the graduations seen around the periphery of reticle which were used to help adjust the weapon depending on the weapon and the range. In the case here, the reticle has been turned to the setting for the 75mm gun at a range of 200 meters. The two reticles were mechanically linked and by rotating the reticle, the gunner moved the center aiming reticle, forcing him to elevate the gun to compensate for range.

usual 75mm Panzergranatpatrone KwK, this gun could penetrate 41mm at 100 meters and 38mm at 500 meters at a 60 degree angle of impact. This was not adequate to knock out the Char B1 bis unless it made a lucky hit on the track or another vulnerable spot. A new shaped-charge, anti-tank round, the Granatpatrone 38 H1/A, could penetrate 70mm, but it was not available for the 1940 fighting. Both tanks also had co-axial machine guns, a 7.92mm MG34 on the PzKpfw IV, and a Riebel 7.5mm MAC31 machine gun on the Char B1 bis.

The Char B1 bis also had a 47mm SA 35 gun in the turret with a co-axial 7.5mm Riebel machine gun. The French 47mm gun had a length of L/32, and did not share the same tube or ammunition as the longer 47mm Mle. 1937 (L/52) towed anti-tank gun. Nevertheless, the 47mm tank gun had an initial muzzle velocity of 670m/s and could penetrate any German tank armor of the campaign at any normal combat range. Main gun ammunition between both tank types were similar, 74 rounds of 75mm on the Char B1 bis and 80 rounds on the PzKpfw IV; the Char B1 bis had an advantage with 50 rounds of 47mm ammunition.

Although the Char B1 bis had better firepower in terms of basic ballistics, it had troublesome fire controls. The task of aiming the main gun was assigned to the driver who had to both steer the tank and aim the 75mm gun. The tank commander had the task of both directing the tank and loading and aiming the 47mm gun. The rate of fire of the 47mm gun was theoretically 15rpm but in practice it was closer to 2–3rpm. Details of this complex fire control system are described in more detail in the crew section below.

The fire controls in the PzKpfw IV were considerably more modern and convenient. The commander was free of responsibilities to tend to the gun, and could concentrate on locating targets and coordinating the actions of his tank with that of neighboring tanks or infantry.

Although the Naeder device offered precise steering to aim the gun, it was often the source of mechanical misfortune during the 1940 campaign due to its fragility and high maintenance demands. "Var" (no. 323) of 2/37e BCC, 1e DCR, was commanded by Lt. de Larmigniere and suffered a breakdown of its Naeder in the town of Ermeton-sur-Biert on May 14, 1940, where it was subsequently abandoned due to a lack of recovery vehicles. (NARA)

The PzKpfw IV was armed with the short 75mm KwK 37 gun which was intended to provide high-explosive fire support and not primarily for tank-vs.-tank fighting. This is the PzKpfw IV Ausf. A command tank of Oberstleutnant Koppenburg, commander of I./Pz.Rgt.1, 1.Panzer Division, near Belfort on June 19, 1940, towards the end of the France campaign. Koppenburg's previous PzKpfw IV was destroyed during the 1939 Poland campaign. (NARA)

MOBILITY

The Char B1 bis was powered by a Renault 6-cylinder aviation engine offering 307 horsepower. It was slower than the PzKpfw IV with a road speed of 25km/h (15mph) compared to 40km/h (25mph). Historians have mocked the Char B1 bis as vulnerable to fuel exhaustion, but the problem was more a tactical and training issue than a technical one. The controversy was so acute that the French Assemblée Nationale had the three armored division commanders testify on the matter to the postwar 1947 investigative commission on the war.

Char B1 bis fuel capacity was 400 liters in a main tank and two supplementary tanks. French press accounts claimed that some crews were unaware of the reserve

The Char B1 bis used a plate-tractor track reminiscent of World War I designs. The suspension was a conventional spring design, hardly evident under all the armor. "Roland" (no. 738), as seen here, was one of the final production Char B1 bis completed at the AMX plant and was delivered to the newly formed 352e CACC at Satory on June 7, 1940. It was rushed into combat, taking part in the fighting near Pazy in the Eure region on June 11, and was scuttled by its crew after running out of fuel in Baccon on June 17, 1940. (Patton Museum)

tanks resulting in fuel exhaustion, but the divisional commanders derided this claim in their testimonies. Fuel consumption was nominally 60 liters per hour, though in practice it was closer to 75 liters per hour. As a result, nominal endurance was between six and eight hours between fueling. However, in practice it was closer to five hours since the crew tended to keep the motor running to prevent the castor oil in the Naeder steering system from congealing and to keep the batteries charged for the radio and turret traverse motor. Fuel consumption was 283 liters per 100km on roads and 410 liters cross-country for a maximum range of 95–140km (60–90 miles). One of the main logistical issues with the engine was its need for high-octane aviation gasoline, not commercial automotive gasoline.

The original Char B1 was equipped with a supply trailer which carried a further 800 liters of fuel and so extended the tank's endurance to about 21–30 hours. This practice was abandoned on the Char B1 bis due to the obvious vulnerability of the trailer, and instead, each tank battalion was supported by 18 TRC Lorraine 37L (*tracteurs de ravitaillement chenillés*) which towed a fuel trailer containing 565 liters of fuel. These were deployed on a scale of six Lorraine tractors per company of 10 tanks. Due to their protracted production, some of the newer units had an insufficient number of tractors; the 3e DCr hadn't received theirs prior to the German attack. A second problem was the time-consuming nature of refueling. Nominally, the pump on the trailer could refill a Char B1 bis in 15 minutes, but in actual practice it was more typically 40–60 minutes. Since there were two tractors for every three tanks, it usually took two hours to conduct a refueling operation. The tractors were supported by fuel tanker trucks at company level which carried a further 3,600 liters of fuel. There were additional fuel reserves at battalion level, and a Char B1 bis battalion nominally had the fuel to last four days on hand at the start of the campaign. In spite of these prudent plans, fuel shortages were a significant cause of Char B1 bis losses in the 1940 France campaign as tanks ran out of fuel during missions, either because the tractors couldn't reach them in time or they simply ran out of fuel themselves. The armored divisions were so new that refueling procedures had not been adequately worked out; the second part of the field manual released at the end of April 1940 dealt with the issue in very general terms, and the third and fourth parts which dealt with the issue in more detail weren't released until May 1940 and were not widely distributed. Barring formal procedures, the lack of time to conduct divisional maneuvers before the war left the divisional staff without sufficient experience to appreciate the problems. During the 1940 campaign, the divisional headquarters tended to keep most of the vulnerable fuel resources in the rear under divisional control to prevent their loss, and these units often became separated from the tank companies when the approach routes roads were clogged with refugees. The battalion commanders were well aware of the range issue and became anxious after a few hours of road march, a common syndrome dubbed the "*Drame du rayon d'action*" (Drama of range) by one of the battalion commanders.

The PzKpfw IV had a Maybach HL 108 TR V-12 gasoline engine offering 250 horsepower. It carried somewhat more fuel than the Char B1 bis, 453 liters in three

The Char B1 bis powertrain included the Renault 307 CV engine (A), and the Naeder servo-motor (B) used for precise control of the transmission (C) for steering the tank and aiming the 75mm hull gun. (Author's collection)

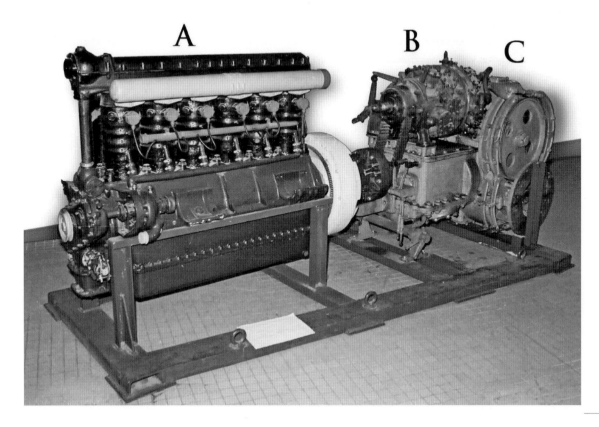

The PzKpfw IV Ausf. D used a conventional spring suspension that offered good, though not exceptional, performance in rough terrain. It was a simple and proven approach compared to the more novel and ambitious torsion bar suspension selected for its stablemate, the PzKpfw III. This is a PzKpfw IV Ausf. D of 4./Pz.Rgt.1, 1.Panzer Division near Sevrance in Alsace on June 21, 1940, at the end of the France campaign. (NARA)

internal tanks. Unlike the Char B1 bis, it operated on ordinary automotive gasoline. Fuel consumption was 318 liters per 100km on road and 500 liters per 100km off-road for a range of 90–140km (55–85 miles) which was similar to the Char B1 bis. Another advantage of the PzKpfw IV was the provision of a separate auxiliary motor that was used to keep the batteries charged, when the tank engine was off, to power the radio, crew intercom and other electrical devices.

German panzer companies lacked a dedicated refueling vehicle comparable to the French Lorraine but did not suffer from a high rate of losses due to fuel exhaustion during the 1940 campaign. This was not due so much to organizational or equipment advantages but rather to tactical experience. The panzer divisions concentrated their fuel supply at divisional level in the division's supply echelon (*Nachschub*) which included three heavy fuel truck companies, an increase in one company since the 1939 Poland campaign. As a result, divisional capacity amounted to 75,000 liters of fuel. The 1938 drive on Vienna and the 1939 Poland campaign had both made it abundantly clear that an ample fuel supply was essential to fast-moving panzer operations. The solution was to reinforce the divisional fuel supply of the lead panzer divisions using several corps-level truck transport battalions, which supplied the panzer spearheads, and to conduct extensive pre-positioning of fuel. The Wehrmacht made extensive use of both 200 liter fuel drums and five liter jerricans that could be carried by any type of truck; fuel pumps were amply distributed to ensure rapid refueling.

THE COMBATANTS

THE CHAR B1 BIS CREW

The Char B1 bis had a crew of four. The crew layout of the Char B1 bis was unusually demanding and required an exceptionally well-trained crew. A US Army attaché granted access to a Char B1 unit before the war concluded that it would take six months to bring a crew to proficiency. One of the most significant differences between the French and German armies was the amount of tank crew training. Both armies relied on the draft, but the French conscription lasted only one year compared to two years for German soldiers. After this, French soldiers had reserve responsibilities, and a large fraction of the Char B1 bis crews were reservists called back to service. However, few reservists had trained on the Char B1 bis when assigned to their units in 1939–40 since so few units had the type until 1940; most had trained on the old and completely different Renault FT. Only the first three battalions had some of their tanks delivered before the outbreak of the war in September 1939, and more than half of the Char B1 bis tanks deployed in May 1940 had only been delivered between two and four months earlier, which restricted the amount of training possible. The French practice was to assign professional soldiers as commanders and drivers since these were the most demanding tasks.

The tank commander (*chef de char*) was usually an officer and he was stationed in the turret of the tank. Inside the turret, he sat on a bicycle-type seat mounted to an elevating post attached to the floor. The commander also had a hatch at the right rear of the turret that folded open to create a seat. It permitted the commander to sit outside the tank during travel when not in the combat zone, but it was not intended

The crew layout of the Char B1 bis. (Author's collection)

for his use in combat since he was so exposed. The commander of the Char B1 bis was overwhelmed with responsibilities since in addition to his command functions, he was also responsible for loading, aiming, and firing the 47mm turret gun and co-axial 7.5mm machine gun. Turret traverse was manual or electric, 28 seconds for full traverse in electric mode and 55 seconds by hand. The electric mode was usually used only when the tank engine was running since it drew so much electrical power.

The commander's vision devices such as the episcopes and binocular periscope in the turret cupola were good. The commander's cupola included three separate vision

The Char B1 bis commander had an exit hatch on the rear of the turret where he could ride when not in the combat zone. However, this position was too exposed for use in combat, and the vision cupola on the roof of the turret lacked a hatch. This is a preserved Char B1 bis at the armor museum at Saumur, home of the French Army's cavalry school and tank training center. (Author's collection)

CHAR B1 BIS TURRET

1. 75mm hull ready ammunition rack (left side)
2. Commander's turret traverse system
3. PPL RX 160 episcope
4. 7.5mm Riebel machine gun
5. L.762 telescopic sight
6. Commander's viewing cupola
7. 47mm SA 35 gun
8. Driver's L.710 binocular gun-sight
9. Driver's steering/aiming wheel
10. 75mm SA 35 tank gun
11. Driver's seat
12. 75mm Obus explosif Mle 1915 (HE)
13. 75mm Obus de rupture Mle 1910M (APHE)

devices including a PPL RX 160 episcope (68 degree field-of-view (FOV)), an Estienne slit under an armored flap (114 degrees FOV), and a four-power binocular periscope. After having located the target, the commander then had to switch to the guns' four-power L.762 telescopic sight which was located immediately above the machine gun and which was common to both weapons. There were two additional PPL RX 160 episcopes on either side of the turret.

In contrast to the German practice, the commander's station in the Char B1 bis was not designed to permit outside observation in combat. The cupola on the turret had no hatch, and the turret hatch left the commander too exposed to be used in combat. As a consequence of the poor turret layout, French tanks tended to operate in a more sluggish fashion than their German adversaries. German accounts of the 1940 fighting invariably characterize the French tank operations as slow, hesitant, and uncoordinated. This was largely due to the various distractions that consumed much of the commander's attention. It's worth noting that these reports were echoed in later accounts of Russian tank operations in 1941–42. In the Soviet case, the tanks had two-man turrets with the commander serving as gunner or loader, with similar distractions from his command functions.

The second most important crewman was the driver (*mécanicien pilote*) who was usually an NCO. He was also overburdened with chores since he not only had to steer the tank, but he also had to aim the main 75mm gun based on the commander's instructions. The driver had two vision devices, a monocular periscopic sight mounted in the overhead hatch with 180 degree coverage, and a PPL RX 160 episcope in front which could be swung open for direct vision. To aim the gun, the driver had a separate L.710 binocular gun-sight located immediately in front of him beneath the episcope.

The driver in the Char B1 bis also aimed the main SA 35 75mm gun. The binocular L.710 sight can be seen immediately above the steering wheel and beneath the open visor port. (Author's collection)

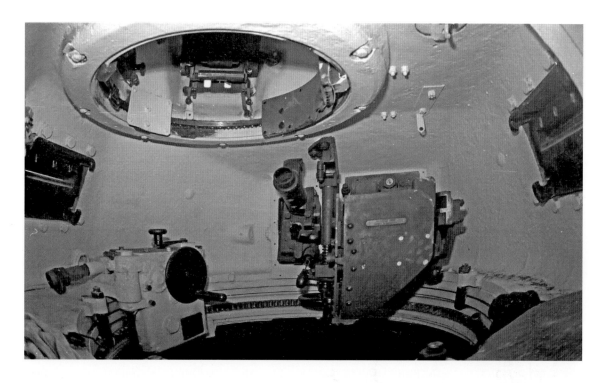

Although French tank units nominally trained the drivers to fire on the move, in practice this was viewed as a waste of ammunition except at extremely short ranges. The usual practice was to fire from the halt, and the driver used the Naeder servo-motor system to fine steer the tank in order to traverse the gun. Elevation was by means of a conventional mechanical elevating wheel which the driver operated using his right hand. The Char B1 bis had a simple voice tube for communication between the commander and driver as well as a set of electric lights for conveying simple commands. A US military attaché who tested a Char B1 before the war thought that the communication system was good, but that the usual practice with French crews was for the commander to direct his steering by means of foot taps on the driver's shoulder.

The third crewman, usually a corporal, was designated as an assistant driver (*mécanicien aide-pilote*) seated behind the 75mm gun. His responsibility was to load the 75mm gun as well as to assist the tank commander by passing him 47mm and machine gun ammunition. Ready-ammunition racks were placed near the main gun, and the rest of the ammunition was scattered through the tank. The engine in the Char B1 bis was off-center to the left, and as a result, there was a narrow corridor on the right rear side of the hull which was used for access to the engine as well as for additional ammunition stowage in the floor and on the side.

The fourth crewman, who was the radio operator, sat behind the driver and directly underneath the commander. The Char B1 bis initially was fitted with an ER 53 transmitter-receiver located in the left side of the hull behind the driver. This radio was adopted in 1933 and operated only in telegraphic fashion by Morse code with no voice capability. Not only did this radio require a skilled operator, but it placed an added burden on the overtaxed commander since messages were generally sent in

The commander in the Char B1 bis stood to the left of the 47mm gun, and operated the turret traverse mechanism with his left hand. The gun breech in this view is obscured by a protective shield which has been folded inward. The commander could conduct surveillance from the vision cupola above, or through the two PPL RX 160 episcopes on either side of the turret. In this photograph, taken inside a restored example, the co-axial Riebel 7.5mm machine gun fitted to the left of the gun and below the L.762 telescopic sight is missing. (Author's collection)

33

some form of code to speed transmission. This radio was obviously unsatisfactory and after only a hundred were manufactured, the "second generation" ER 51 Mle. 1938 entered production. This set had both telegraphic and voice transmission with a range of about 10km in telegraphic mode and about 2–3km in voice mode. Command tanks had an additional radio.

Although the Char B1 bis had four men on board the tank, the crew assigned to each tank was usually six or seven. The other crewman were classified as "Graisseurs" (*Greasers*) since the tank required up to six hours of maintenance per day with special attention needed for engine oil, lubrication of the suspension and other parts, and maintaining the oil supply in the delicate Naeder steering mechanism. These additional crewman traveled in the battalion's support echelon. In some units, one of the *graisseurs* was carried in the tank to assist the commander by passing up ammunition; this was a help in combat but the fighting compartment of the Char B1 bis was quite crowded with a fifth crewman.

PZKPFW IV CREW

The PzKpfw IV crew was larger than that of the Char B1 bis, with five men: three in the turret and two in the hull. The PzKpfw IV had a turret basket with rotating floor. The tank commander (*Kommandant*) sat on "the throne" in the rear center of the turret behind the main gun. As mentioned earlier, both the PzKpfw III and PzKpfw

The crew layout of the PzKpfw IV Ausf. D. (Author's collection)

PZKPFW IV TURRET

1. Commander's seat
2. Gunner's seat
3. Gunner's elevating and traverse hand-wheels
4. Gunner's azimuth indicator
5. Gunner's TZF5b telescopic sight
6. 75mm KwK 37
7. Turret ventilator
8. 7.92mm MG34 co-axial machine gun
9. Loader's seat
10. Turret basket floor
11. 7.5cm High Explosive
12. 7.5cm Armor-Piercing (Capped)

IV were fitted with a special vision cupola that had been inspired by the experiments at Kazan. The cupola had five vision ports that were shielded externally by armored visors, and then shielded again by 50mm thick bullet-resistant glass. In addition, the cupola had an overhead split hatch which allowed the commander to operate with his head out of the tank for better situational awareness. The commander communicated with the rest of the crew through a vehicle intercom system using a throat mike that was a generation more advanced than the French counterpart.

The gunner (*Richtkanonier*) was located in the left side of the turret. The main gun was aimed using a TZF5b telescopic sight. Traverse and elevation were undertaken with mechanical hand cranks. The traverse could be operated at two speeds, a higher speed, coarse setting, and a fine setting for precise adjustments.

This is one of the iconic images of the Blitzkrieg era as it was widely used in German propaganda, including on the cover of *Signal* magazine. It shows a decorated veteran of the Poland campaign, Lt. Günther, of 4./Pz.Rgt.9, 10.Panzer Division, during exercise as the Baumholder training ground in April 1940, shortly before the France campaign. The bison insignia was the symbol of Pz.Rgt.9 and the rhomboid plate below that indicates the 4th company, 3rd platoon, 2nd tank. (NARA)

There were five crew members in the PzKpfw IV Ausf. D as seen during these training exercises of Pz.Rgt.9, 10.Panzer Division at Baumholder in April 1940. (NARA)

The loader (*Ladekanonier*) had a seat on the right side of the turret but in action the seat would be folded and the loader would stand on the turret basket floor. The ammunition was scattered about the fighting compartment in bins on the floor and in the side sponsons with 34 rounds immediately around the loader. The gunner was also responsible for loading the co-axial machine gun which was directly in front of him.

The driver (*Fahrer*) was located in the left front of the hull. Steering was a conventional Wilson clutch-steering type manufactured by Krupp with the transmission in the front center of the hull and the steering brakes forward of the driver. The driver had a direct-vision port with armored cover immediately in front of him protected by thick glass, and when this was closed during combat, he had a KFF binocular periscope that operated through two small apertures in the armor plate above the visors.

The radio operator (*Funker*) sat in the right front hull opposite the driver. The FuG5 radio transmitter-receiver was mounted centrally above the transmission to the left of the radio-operator. This was a fairly modern voice/telegraphic AM radio with an effective range of about 2km in voice mode.

CREW TRAINING

The Combat-Duel section to follow will focus on the clash at Stonne on May 15–16, 1940, so the focus here is on the specific training of the opposing units, Pz.Rgt.8 of the 10.Panzer Division and the 41e and 49e BCC of the 5e Demi-brigade Lourde of the 3e DCr. The German Army had a notable advantage in crew experience and in training due to earlier mobilization and the lessons of the Poland campaign. Besides combat lessons, the Poland campaign also underlined the vital importance of many routine tasks such as the refueling issue discussed earlier.

A fine study of "Vauquois" (no 372) of the 41e BCC during training, in the spring of 1940, under the command of Lt. Jacques Hachet. It took part in the battle at Stonne as part of 3/41e BCC and remained in action until May 20 when it suffered a mechanical breakdown. (NARA)

Pz.Rgt.8 had been formed as part of the third batch of new panzer regiments in the autumn of 1936, three years ahead of its future French opponents. It was built around cadre units from Pz.Rgt.3 and Pz.Rgt.5, which each provided one company of the eight in the regiment, making up a quarter of its new strength. The Panzertruppen were an elite force chosen for mechanical aptitude and had second priority in the Wehrmacht after the Luftwaffe. The regiment was initially equipped with the PzKpfw I Ausf. A light tank and began to receive the newer PzKpfw I Ausf. B and PzKpfw II in the summer of 1937 during its live-fire exercises at Putlos on the Baltic.

Once its initial formation and training was complete at Zossen in April 1938, it was rotated to its home, Kaserne at Böblingen in Baden. In contrast to the compressed training available to its French opponents, Pz.Rgt.8 enjoyed an ample training regimen which allowed extensive crew cross-training so that if a crewman were injured or wounded in combat, someone else in the crew could take their place. The forested countryside around Böblingen was not spacious enough for large-unit exercise, so the regiment was dispatched to other areas in 1938–39, including the large training grounds at Grafenwöhr near the Czech border. This allowed combined-arms training with artillery and infantry units, as well as a large enough exercise area for long-distance marches to test the ability of the unit to sustain and maintain the tanks. Two years after its own formation in October 1938, the regiment was well enough trained that it was ordered to give up a number of officers to serve as the cadre for newly formed panzer units. By November 1938, enough of the unit's enlisted men had already completed their two-year conscription, and they were rotated out and into the Army reserve and their place was taken by new recruits. Another set of major field exercises were conducted in March 1939 to make certain that the new influx of

TANK ACE: CAPITAINE PIERRE BILLOTTE

Capt. Pierre Bilotte, commander of the Char B1 bis "Eure" during the battle of Stonne on May 16, 1940, had a remarkable career later in the war. Born on March 8, 1906, he was the son of Général d'armée Gaston Billotte who commanded the 1re Groupe d'Armées in May 1940, the French Army group which advanced into Belgium. Pierre Billotte attended the St. Cyr military academy and later the École superieure de guerre (Higher School of War) and commanded the 1e Companie, 41e BCC, in 1940 at Aubigny-sur-Nere. Tank no. 337 "Eure" was built by FCM and was delivered to the 2/41e BCC at the Gien arsenal on December 8, 1939; it was assigned to Billotte's company on May 10 and became his command tank during the fighting. Following the battle of Stonne, Billotte took part in the later fighting of the 41e BCC. His tank, "Eure", was scuttled in Possesse on June 13, 1940, after a power-train failure. Billotte was wounded during the fighting and became a prisoner-of-war. He was sent to an officer camp in Pomerania but managed to escape to the Soviet Union shortly before the German invasion in June 1941. After being interned for a short while, he was assigned as the Free French military attaché to Moscow. He eventually moved to London and served as de Gaulle's Chief of Staff in 1942–43. He requested a combat posting and led the GTV (Groupement Tactique V), a combat command of the 2e Division blindée, which was the lead element in the liberation of Paris in August 1944. He was promoted to

Capt. Pierre Billotte commanded a Char B1 bis named "Eure" during the fighting at Stonne in May 1940, and went on to a have distinguished career with the Free French forces in 1944–45. (Author's Collection)

Général de brigade in September 1944, and after disagreements with the divisional commander, Jacques Leclerc, he was eventually reassigned to head the formation of 10e Division d'infanterie. This was one of a number of new formations created from the FFI (Forces Françaises de l'Intérieur) resistance units. This division was committed to combat in Alsace during the time of Operation *Nordwind* and the liberation of the Colmar pocket in January 1945. After the war, he was the Assistant Chief of Staff of the French Army and headed the French Military Mission to the UN in 1946–50. After his retirement, he became an active politician on the left wing of the Gaullist movement, taking part in the formation of the UDT trade union movement (Union démocratique du travail). He served as the Minister of National Defense in the Edgar Fauré administration (1955–56) and the Minister of Overseas Departments and Territories in the Georges Pompidou administration (1966–68); he was mayor of Créteil in greater Paris from 1965 to 1977. He died in 1992.

recruits had been properly trained. Some of the first wave of conscripts elected to remain in the Army, generally becoming NCOs and taking over more technical tasks on the tank in roles such as gunner or driver. By 1938, the regiment had also seen steady re-equipment with a few of the new PzKpfw III, as well as the PzKpfw IV which equipped one company in each of its two battalions. Pz.Rgt.8 did not take part in either the Austrian Anschluss or the occupation of the Sudentenland, but in April 1939, after having been assigned to the 10.Panzer Division, it was moved to the Milowitz training ground in the occupied Czech republic. When it was alerted for participation in the September 1939 invasion of Poland, its tank strength stood at 162 panzers including 9 Befehlspanzer (command tanks), 57 PzKpfw I, 74 PzKpfw II, 3 PzKpfw III and 7 PzKpfw IV.

During the 1939 Poland campaign, Pz.Rgt.8 crossed the Pomeranian corridor into East Prussia, and then took part in the campaign in eastern Poland, including the siege of the fortress town of Brzesc-nad-Bugiem (Brest-Litovsk). The short campaign was hard on the men and machines, and by the time combat had ceased for the regiment on September 17, when it met the Red Army, it was down to 75 of its original 162 panzers, less than half-strength after fewer than two weeks of fighting. These were not all combat casualties, but included large numbers of breakdowns which would later be recovered. The old and weakly armored PzKpfw I light tanks were particularly hard hit with only 16 operational out of the original 57. Following the campaign, the regiment conducted an extensive discussion of "lessons learned", and underwent an organizational restructuring in February 1940. This was done by reducing the number of obsolete PzKpfw I and incorporating as many of the new PzKpfw III and PzKpfw IV as were available. The PzKpfw III were mixed into the light companies to offer more firepower while the PzKpfw IV were kept together in the two heavy companies. By the time of the French campaign in May 1940, the regimental strength had fallen from the 162 deployed against Poland to 134. However, the regiment now had 45 medium tanks (29 PzKpfw III, 16 PzKpfw IV), many more

A view of the 1/41e BCC on exercise in the spring of 1940. The tank in the foreground is "Vauquois" (no. 377), at the time the tank of the company commander, Capt. Cantarel. During the 1940 fighting it was commanded by Lt. Pierre Bourgeois and it was knocked out by artillery fire near Perthes on June 10, 1940. The tank to the left is "Vertus" (no. 372). (NARA)

than the ten they had in Poland. At the time of the May 1940 attack, Pz.Rgt.8 was fully trained with the vast majority of its crews already combat veterans.

The French Char B1 bis battalions were not as well trained as their German counterparts because they were generally formed quite late due to the slow delivery of the new Char B1 bis tanks. In the case of the Char B1 bis battalions of the 3e DCr, they only started organization on December 5, 1939. In the 49e BCC, the officers were professional soldiers and came from six other prewar tank battalions. The NCOs and enlisted men were mostly reservists whose experience was often limited to the antiquated Renault FT light tank. Shortages of tank crews were a recurrent problem. The 41e BCC, which was supposed to have 706 troops, had only 450 in April and 600 in mid-May 1940 when committed to combat. The 49e BCC was somewhat better off with 634 troops in early April 1940 and close to a full complement by the start of the war. The division's mechanized infantry element, the 16e BCP (Bataillon de chasseurs portés), was pilfered of personnel to fill out the understrength tank battalions, and as a result at the time of the 1940 fighting was barely two companies in strength with about 450 troops instead of 800 men. Training on the Char B1 bis for the 49e BCC did not begin until February 1940 when the unit moved to its station at Argent-sur-Sauldre. Live-fire with the tanks' machine guns began in late February and the first allotments of 75mm training ammunition permitted the first live-fire from the main guns in mid-March 1940. The French had less extensive live-fire ranges for tank guns than the Germans, principally the base at Suippes and a new tank center at Lunéville which was not completed before the outbreak of war. The equipping and training of the 3e DCr was not expected to be completed until the late summer of 1940 and it was missing many vehicles including its Lorraine fuel tractors.

The situation in the division's two Hotchkiss H-39 light tank battalions was similar. The 45e BCC was also known as the 45e BCG (Batallion de chars de la Gendarmerie) as it had been raised late in 1939 from Gendarmerie units, mainly the Garde Républicaine Mobile.

The only Char B1 bis unit to see some action prior to the May 1940 campaign was the 15e BCC stationed near Nancy which took part in the limited French offensive in the Saar, passing through the Maginot Line over the German border near Tunting from September 10 to 22, 1939. The unit was then withdrawn back to France.

THE FRENCH DCR

The French Army was a very enthusiastic proponent of tanks and mechanization, but its armored units were divided between the infantry and cavalry branches, both of which had their own approaches to mechanization. The World War I tank force had emerged from the artillery branch, but after the war it came under the control of the infantry. Tanks had played an important role in the 1918 victory, and so remained a vital element of infantry doctrine. The inspector general of the infantry in 1938 remarked that "My profound conviction is that these machines are destined to play a decisive role in a future conflict; the infantry was unable to do without tanks in the last war and will be able even less in future operations. The tank must be the preferred arm in a nation poor in personnel. War is a question of force where the advantage rests with the most powerful machine and not with the most rapid machine." Even though the French Army was strongly wedded to the tank, this did not lead to an immediate acceptance of the need for armored divisions.

France's development of armored divisions was severely constrained by its profoundly defensive strategic outlook in the 1930s. Infantry tanks were primarily intended to accompany the infantry into battle, much as in 1918, and not to serve as an offensive strike force comparable to German panzer divisions. The principal infantry tank types in 1940 were infantry accompanying tanks such as the Renault R-35 and Hotchkiss H-39 which were strongly armored, slow tanks designed to perform the same function as the Renault FT tank in World War I. The bulk of the French Army's tank force in May 1940 was located in the separate battalions of accompanying tanks and these numbered 1,540 in May 1940, or about half the force.

The French cavalry recognized the failure of horse cavalry in World War I and embraced mechanization more enthusiastically than the infantry to maintain its rationale as the Army's mobile force. In contrast to the infantry tank force, which lacked a powerful proponent of armored divisions after Estienne's retirement in 1927, the cavalry had an important advocate for mechanization in Gén. Maxime Weygand, the Chief of the General Staff and Vice-President of the Superior War Council. After a failed experiment with mixed horse/mechanized units in 1932, the cavalry decided to begin a process of forming mechanized divisions (DLM: Division Légère Méchanique) with the 1e DLM formed in 1935–36, and the 2e DLM in 1937. By the time of the 1940 campaign, three of these divisions were in service. These were modern combined arms formations mixing cavalry tank squadrons, half-track-borne

The combat companion of the Char B1 bis in the DCr were the Hotchkiss H-39 light tanks such as this example from the 25e BCC of the 1e DCR which was lost during the fighting for Avesnes with Rommel's 7.Panzer Division on May 17, 1940. (NARA)

rifle troops and mechanized artillery. The two principal tank types in these formations were the Hotchkiss H-39 and the Somua S-35 and they were supported by the excellent Panhard 178 armored car. The cavalry also embraced mechanization for many of its smaller corps-level reconnaissance regiments, depending primarily on light tanks and armored cars. Even if the cavalry was by far the most modern and progressive element of the Army, it still played a secondary role to the infantry. In May 1940, only about 835, or roughly a quarter, of the Army's tanks were in cavalry units.

The infantry's acceptance of the need for armored divisions was belated and grudging. The Char B1 had been built for the infantry, so its employment was tightly connected with this debate. The Char B1 had been manufactured in a doctrinal vacuum without much consensus within the infantry branch about its role. Estienne had envisioned the Char B as a maneuver tank quite distinct from the infantry accompanying tanks. However, Estienne retired in 1927 before any formal tactical doctrine had been established, and there were no Char B tanks in service beyond a handful of prototypes until the late 1930s. Indeed, the lack of a modern, mobile tank was a primary reason for the infantry's skepticism about large tank formations.

When production of the Char B was finally budgeted for in the mid-1930s, attention began to be paid to the concept of *chars de manoeuvre ensemble* which unlike the accompanying tanks would play a spearhead role ahead of the main wave of infantry. Field trials of the B1 and D2 tanks for the mass maneuver role were conducted at Sissone in April 1937. This role was closer to that of the old Char 2C breakthrough tank tied to the infantry rather than the independent battle tank role envisioned by Estienne when he first proposed the Char B in 1920. Even though these units were not constrained to direct infantry support, they were seen as small, battalion-sized formations that would tactically support infantry divisions but in a more independent fashion than the accompanying tanks.

Tank enthusiasts, such as the retired Estienne as well as younger firebrands like Col. Charles de Gaulle, advocated the consolidation of battle tanks into an offensively oriented division with their own autonomous mission. Through the late 1930s, this idea had little support in the Superior War Council which established French Army policy. As late as 1936, General Gamelin noted that "The problems of constituting large tank units has been studied in France since 1932; the development of the antitank weapon has caused a renunciation of this concept." By 1937, opinions were shifting to the acceptance of heavy tank brigades based on the Char B, but these were still short of a combined-arms division. There was increasing recognition that such units might be useful as a mobile counterattack force against the German panzer divisions. In 1938, the Superior War Council ordered the formation of a commission under the Army's tank inspector to study a large armored unit consisting of two Char B1 battalions, a battalion of Char D2 tanks, two motorized infantry battalions and two motorized artillery battalions. Although field trials were planned, the German annexation of Austria and the Sudeten crisis prompted the French Army to cancel the trials for fear of increasing international tensions. By late 1938, there was a growing appreciation for a division-sized formation with the capability to act autonomously but there was also the conviction that not enough Char B battle tanks would be ready to form such a unit until October 1940 at the earliest and perhaps not until 1941. A provisional manual on the tactical employment of armored divisions was released for comment in February 1939. The tactical doctrine still did not envision the armored division as an autonomous force, but rather as part of an infantry corps to assist in the maneuver of infantry divisions.

The German demonstration of the combat potential of panzer divisions in Poland in 1939 ended the French procrastination about armored divisions. The first step, which began in September 1939, was to create demi-brigades which unified a pair of tank battalions under a common headquarters. Although there was still a shortage of battle tanks, the formation of four armored divisions (DCr: Division Cuirasée) was approved, and the first two, the 1e and 2e DCr, began formation in January 1940 and the 3e DCr followed in March 1940. They were sometimes nicknamed the "Three Bs" due to their commanders: Bruneau, Bruché and Brocard. De Gaulle's 4e DCr was a last-minute improvisation which began forming in May 1940 after the German attack to block the approaches to Paris.

The DCr was smaller and less powerful than a German panzer division and was not a balanced combined arms force. Its main strength resided in a pair of tank demi-brigades split between two battalions of Char B1 bis and two battalions of Hotchkiss H-39. Unlike the panzer division which had one, and sometimes two, regiments of infantry, the DCr had only a battalion of infantry due to the slow production of its Lorraine tracked infantry carriers. The DCr also lacked a mechanized reconnaissance unit due to shortages of armored cars. As a result, the DCr had half the strength of a panzer division: 6,155 men versus over 13,000 men in the larger panzer divisions. Likewise, the tank strength of the DCr was significantly less at about 160 tanks versus an average of 265 tanks in the panzer divisions in May 1940.

Char B1 bis units often suffered casualties after their fuel supply was cut off. This is a column of TRC Lorraine refueling tractors of the 1e DCR which was overrun on May 17, 1940, in Avesnes during an attack by Rommel's 7.Panzer Division.

French Tank Strength, May 1940									
Unit	FT	R-35	H-35/-39	FCM-36	D2	B1 bis	AMR	S-35	Total
1e DCr			90			69			159
2e DCr			90			69			159
3e DCr			90			62			152
4e DCr		135	35		45	33		35	283
1e Armée*		90	90						180
2e Armée*		45		90					135
3e Armée*	120	180							300
4e Armée*	60	90							150
5e Armée*	60	135							195
7e Armée*		90							90
8e Armée*	120	90							210
9e Armée*	60	90							150
Armée des Alpes*	60								60
Compagnies autonome (June)	40		30		40	(53)			163
1e DLM			92				56	96	244
2e DLM			92				58	96	246
3e DLM			80					80	160
1e–5e DLC			48				115		163
1e–7e GRDI			16				8		24
Deployed	520	945	753	90	85	233	237	307	3,170

*Tank battalions attached to the field army

The cavalry's counterpart of the Char B1 bis was the Somua S-35. This used the APX-1 CE turret which was similar to the APX-4 on the Char B1 bis and armed with the same gun. Although widely regarded as the best French tank of 1940, it shared the problem of having a one-man turret. This particular tank served in the 2e DLM, was captured by the Germans and turned over to the Italian Army, and then captured again by the US Army near Rome. It is seen here after restoration at the Ordnance Museum at Aberdeen Proving Ground, Maryland. (Author's collection)

Aside from organizational weakness, the belated organization of these divisions significantly reduced their battlefield effectiveness. The divisional components had little, if any, combined training and many of the component elements were newly formed or newly equipped due to the late start of the French rearmament program. The six Char B1 bis battalions in the first three DCr were not fully equipped until the spring of 1940. Supplies of the Lorraine tractor for the Chasseur Portés infantry battalions were extremely late, if they arrived at all before the start of the campaign.

Combined training was quite limited. The 1re DCr was consolidated in towns around the Champagne camp in the Suippes area and had about three months of training before the start of the war. However, this was limited to small-unit training with little integrated divisional training. The 2e DCr was consolidated in the towns around Haute Moivre and, like the 1e DCr, underwent about three months of training including specialized tank training at the neighboring Mourmelon camp. On May 8, just days before the start of the war, the 2e DCr conducted an exercise to simulate a counterattack on an enemy force. The mechanized cavalry advocate, Général Jean Flavigny, witnessed the exercise and was disheartened to see that it took the division four hours to move four kilometers and that even once it reached its objective, the division was completely disorganized. The 3e DCr was consolidated around Reims but had less than a month of combined training prior to the start of the war. This unit faced the greatest challenge since its new Char B1 bis tanks were the last to arrive.

Beyond the training limitations of the DCr, their combat use was further hampered by the inexperience of senior commanders in employing them. While infantry corps commanders were well versed in Army doctrine on the use of the accompanying tank battalions, the DCr were an entirely new type of unit with a very different combination of capabilities and limitations than those of a conventional infantry division with tank support.

THE PANZER DIVISIONS

Many officers in the Reichswehr became convinced that tanks were the wave of the future and could restore offensive operations in land warfare. In spite of the Versailles treaty ban, the Reichswehr began initial steps in the clandestine formation of mechanized units. Much of the initiative for these efforts came from the Army's motorization department, which began by examining the role of the truck in the tactical movement of infantry troops, but which concluded that tanks were a vital necessity in future land warfare. Agitation for the panzer force came especially from the office of the Inspector for Motorized Troops (Inspektür für Heeres-motorisierung) headed after 1931 by Generalmajor Oswald Lutz and his Chief of Staff, Oberstleutnant Heinz Guderian. Lutz was the architect of the early panzer force, but Guderian became its most vocal proponent and the key advocate of the panzer's tactical and operational potential. The Reichswehr's extensive contacts with the Red Army in the 1920s further encouraged an interest in tank warfare. The Russian Front in World War I had not congealed into static trench warfare and the Russian Civil War had seen extensive use of armored vehicles, though mainly armored cars and armored trains rather than tanks. The Red Army was in the forefront of mechanization efforts and had the most active tank production program in Europe in the late 1920s and early 1930s.

Tanks fit comfortably into German offensive tactics which were based on the lessons of the Great War. The prominent role played by specialized assault infantry using infiltration tactics paved the way for a more radical version substituting tanks;

During the France campaign of 1940, the panzer divisions were still heavily dependent on light tanks such as the PzKpfw I, seen in the center here, and the more adequate PzKpfw II, seen to the right. After the Poland campaign, many of the PzKpfw I tanks were retired due to their thin armor and inadequate firepower. However, they remained in use for training as shown here with Pz.Rgt.9, 10.Panzer Division at the Baumholder training grounds in April 1940. (NARA)

panzer divisions could take this one step beyond and use infiltration at an operational level. Hitler's accession to power in 1933, and the subsequent Nazi remilitarization program, provided the momentum and money for mechanization. The German Army was starting from a clean slate and the infantry branch was far less obstructive in the formation of large panzer units than was the case in France. While there was the usual conservative resistance to such expensive novelties, Hitler's political radicalism included an enthusiasm for military futurism that enthusiastically supported the budgetary demands of the Army's visionary thinkers. On seeing an early demonstration of PzKpfw I tanks, Hitler blurted out "That's what I want!"

The first panzer unit was clandestinely created at Zossen, in November 1933, as an experimental training unit, and the tables for an experimental panzer division were distributed within the Army in October 1934. Guderian pressed for the manufacture of medium tanks and gun support tanks like the ZW and BW, but Lutz prudently recommended production of the adequate and available Pzkpfw I to provide immediate resources for training and tactical experimentation. In January 1935, Lutz recommended the formation of the first three panzer divisions and three panzer brigades. Hitler also urged motorization of the cavalry, and so the proposed panzer brigades were converted from horse cavalry regiments. The general staff recommended that a panzer regiment be raised to support each of the infantry divisions, but it was recognized that this was unrealistic in view of the large number of tanks required and the limited industrial resources. As a step in that direction, the proposal was trimmed to the creation of a panzer regiment for each of the 12 Army corps.

By the summer of 1935, there were 300 PzKpfw I in service, and this permitted the organization of the first panzer division near Munster, with two more following as more tanks became available. Cavalry mechanization expanded from original plans and turned instead to the creation of the Light Division (Leichte Division) which was intended for traditional cavalry roles such as reconnaissance and exploitation but which lacked the full offensive power of the panzer division for decisive battle. By 1938, five panzer divisions and four light divisions had been organized. The absorption of the Sudetenland and the Czech Republic in 1938–39 provided an

The panzer division was intended to be a combined arms team, but the mechanization of the infantry was slow. The battle of France saw the combat debut of the Sd.Kfz. 251 half-track infantry transporter, but it was still scarce and supplied to only a handful of units. This is a Mannschafts-transportwagen Sd.Kfz 251 Ausf. B with 9./Schützen Brigade.5 of the 5.Panzer Division on exercise at the Baumholder training grounds in April 1940. (NARA)

German Tank Strength, May 1940								
Unit	PzKpfw I	PzKpfw II	PzKpfw 35(t)	PzKpfw 38(t)	PzKpfw III	PzKpfw IV	Befelspanzer	Total
1.Pz. Div.	24	115			62	48	23	272
2.Pz. Div.	24	158			86	20	*	288
3.Pz. Div.	109	122			29	20	*	280
4.Pz. Div.	160	107			44	32	23	366
5.Pz. Div.	75	116			35	32	*	258
6.Pz. Div.		50	106			26	10	192
7.Pz. Div.	37	72		48		23	*	180
8.Pz. Div.		15		180		30	*	225
9.Pz. Div.	28	72			45	11	*	156
10.Pz. Div.	66	128			48	36	*	278
Deployed strength	523	955	106	228	349	278	220	2,659
Available strength	1,077	1,092	143	238	381	290	244	3,465
Losses 5-6/40	182	240	45	54	135	97	69	822

*Complete data on command tanks not available

unexpected increase in tank strength by absorbing the Czech tanks as the PzKpfw 35(t) and 38(t). In February 1939, the general staff decided to convert the light divisions into the more versatile panzer divisions in the autumn of 1939, but the Poland campaign intervened before this change was implemented.

The successful use of the panzer divisions in Poland in September 1939 led to further maturation of tactical doctrine and a further concentration of the panzer units. In the wake of the campaign, the general staff agreed that the separate panzer regiments under corps command would be used to reinforce the panzer divisions. For the France campaign, the panzer divisions were further concentrated into corps formations, with generally two panzer divisions per corps and in the case of the main effort on the Meuse, three corps were unified under a single expedient armored group, Panzergruppe Kliest.

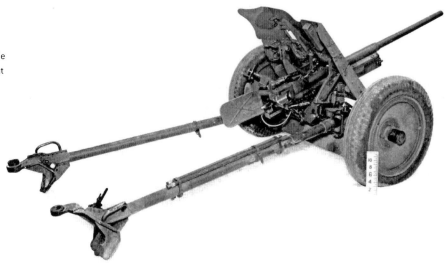

Gen. Charles Delestraint, who led the French armored counterattack at Abbeville in 1940, later complained that "We had 3,000 tanks and so did the Germans. We used them in a thousand packets of three and the Germans in three packs of a thousand." This criticism of the French use of "penny-packets" of tanks has become a cliché for the misuse of French armor in 1940, but it confuses several critical issues. The excessive concentration of the German panzer force in 1940 was partly due to the radical "Case Yellow" plan which required a highly concentrated mobile force to quickly move through the Ardennes. The German Army had long expected to provide tanks to support the infantry at divisional or corps level, but simply did not have enough to go around in 1940. The German Army never again concentrated its panzer force as tightly as in 1940. Over the subsequent years of war, the German Army, like most other major armies, gradually dispersed the armored force to provide infantry divisions and corps with armored support in the form of organic assault gun companies, tank-destroyer companies and battalions, and heavy tank regiments.

The French Army had half of its tank force concentrated in the DCr and DLM, which was not an abnormal dispersion by later World War II standards. For example, the US Army had 48 of its 118 tank battalions in armored divisions in 1944, about 40 percent of its tanks, and this percentage would be even smaller if the self-propelled tank destroyer battalions were counted in the tally. Likewise, the Red Army in 1944 had about 40 percent of its tanks and self-propelled guns in its tank and mechanized corps while the majority served in separate armored regiments and battalions to support the rifle and cavalry divisions. The French did concentrate their DLM in Gen. René Prioux's cavalry corps and used it to considerable effect in the early days of the campaign in the battles for the Gembloux gap.

The problem that the French Army faced in 1940 was not the number of armored divisions, but their late formation, lack of training, incomplete equipment and immature doctrine. The French art of war in 1940 was far less compatible with armored warfare than German practices. The French doctrine in 1940 focused on methodical battle with an emphasis on fire and protection with the expectation of a prolonged war of attrition closer in tempo to 1918 than 1939. The German art of war in 1940 sought a decisive battle of annihilation with an emphasis on shock and surprise and which intended a fast battle tempo as in Poland in 1939.

At the tactical level, German practices were more compatible with the use of tanks as a maneuver force. To deal with the chaos of modern war, the Germans practiced *Auftragstaktik*, a decentralized approach to command-and-control. This was based on the notion that the tactical commander should be issued orders which clearly identified the intent of the mission but did not precisely dictate the method to obtain the objective. Such a command style demanded exceptional initiative from tactical commanders. The French preferred methodical battle, a tactical style that favored centralized command and micro-management of the tactical commanders from higher commands. It discouraged initiative at lower command levels, and made officers dependent on the receipt of orders from higher commands before initiating actions.

Not only did the German Army expect the pace of war to be much faster in 1940 than in 1914–18, they expected to exploit this pace through more advanced means of command-and-control. The Germans went to great lengths to deploy tactical radios as extensively as the technology would permit. Radio was part of the revolution in military affairs that is often called Blitzkrieg. For the first time, it provided commanders with the means to obtain reconnaissance and operational information in near real-time. The French Army also attempted to deploy tactical radios, but lacked the doctrinal impetus to overcome the substantial cost and technological problems. Only about half of French tanks had radios, while virtually all German tanks had at least receivers.

Although most of the German panzer strength was in the panzer divisions in 1940, the battle of France saw the first steps in deepening the Army's mechanization through the development of infantry support vehicles such as the StuG III Ausf. A assault gun seen here. At the time, only a few dozen of these had been manufactured and this example served in the elite Großdeutschland Regiment which would see combat at Stonne a few days later. This is the traffic jam on the D5 route in Floing on May 13 when Guderian's corps began its attempts to jump the Meuse near Sedan. To the right is a Mannschafts-transportwagen Sd.Kfz 251 Ausf. B of 10./Schützen Regiment.1. (NARA)

THE STRATEGIC SITUATION

When Army Group B lunged into the Netherlands and Belgium at the start of the campaign, the French Army responded by surging into Belgium. A major tank battle ensued around the Gembloux gap when Prioux's cavalry corps threw is mechanized cavalry units into the fray. These Somua S-35 cavalry tanks of the 2e Cuirassiers, 3e DLM, were knocked out during the fighting with the 4.Panzer Division at Merdorp near Hannut, on May 13, during engagements with Pz.Rgt.35, 4.Panzer Division. (NARA)

The rapid defeat of France in 1940 was one of the most shocking military calamities in modern European history, paralleled by the Prussian catastrophe at Jena in 1806 at the hands of Napoleon. The roots of this defeat are complex and have been the subject of considerable historical controversy ever since.

French military policy in the late 1930s was aimed at avoiding defeat rather than at victory over Germany. Bled white by the Great War, and substantially overmatched by German economic power, France created the impressive Maginot Line defenses,

Prior to reaching the Meuse, Guderian's corps had to cross the Semois river at Bouillon. Here, a PzKpfw I Ausf. B of the 1.Panzer Division begins to ford the Semois on May 12. German engineers had completed a trestle bridge, shown in the background, that day, but it was not sufficient for tank traffic. (NARA)

along the Moselle in Lorraine and along the Rhine in Alsace, as a centerpiece of its defensive strategy. The fortifications petered out before reaching the Belgian border due to both a lack of funds and a mistaken conviction that the Ardennes presented an insurmountable geographic barrier to German invasion. The Maginot Line was intended to limit Germany's offensive options, and force the German Army to choose the predictable route through the Netherlands and Belgium. French strategic planning assumed that the Germans would dust off the Schlieffen Plan from 1914, and as a result developed their own response, called Plan D, or the Dyle Plan, after the river where the main defense line would be established. With the Netherlands and Belgium neutral, the French Army and the allied British Expeditionary Force would have to wait for the German attack. When Dutch and Belgian neutrality were violated, the Allies could lunge forward into Belgium, establishing a firm defensive line along the Dyle river. This plan was undermined by a later decision to extend the line towards the Netherlands on the Breda river. It was renamed the Dyle-Breda Plan. This extension forced the French Army to commit its reserve force into Belgium, denying the French commanders a counterattack force should the Germans do something unexpected. Mobility was the key to this plan, and the French forces assigned to Plan D included its only ready mobile force, the cavalry's DLM in the Prioux cavalry corps.

Indeed, the German Army originally did dust off the Schlieffen Plan and intended to crush their way through the Netherlands and Belgium in a mechanized variant of 1914. The most vocal opponent of this plan was the erstwhile Chief of Staff of Army Group A, Erich von Manstein. He argued that such a plan simply allowed the French to push their best units into the narrow Belgian corridor and risked another grotesque stalemate as had occurred in 1914–18. With the new panzer force available, Manstein suggested a far riskier gamble. As in a bull-fight, Army Group B would unfurl the red matador's cape to entice the Allies' armored bull forward. By exploiting to French and

The crossing of the Meuse by Guderian's panzer corps was the critical first phase of the "Sickle Cut" maneuver. Here, a PzKpfw II Ausf. B light tank of 4./Pz.Rgt.1, 1.Panzer Division, crosses the Meuse in the northern suburbs of Sedan over a pontoon bridge on May 14, 1940. The village of Glaire is in the background on the opposite bank. The battle for Stonne, which started the following day, was prompted by this bridgehead. (NARA)

British preconceptions, the bulk of the best Allied forces would be lured deep into Belgium. The matador's sword would then come from an unexpected direction. Army Group A with most of the panzer force would quickly slip through the Ardennes in Luxembourg, and exit near Sedan on the Meuse river where the Maginot Line largely ended. Army Group A would then be behind the main Allied force, and a race to the Channel would trap them. Manstein's plan was an enormous risk since prompt Allied action could blunt the advance out of the Ardennes. However, Manstein's assessment was that the Allied coalition forces would be sluggish in the opening phase of the campaign, and provide the critical time needed for Army Group A to make an unopposed deep penetration to Sedan and beyond.

The Char B1 bis of the 1e DCr became entangled with German tanks of Army Group B. "Verdun II" (no. 452) was the command tank of Général de Brigade Bruneau, commander of the 1e Demi-brigade Lourde of the 1e DCR, hence the two stars on the turret. On May 16, the unit became heavily engaged with Rommel's 7.Panzer Division around Avesnes, and this tank was knocked out late that evening due to a shell hit to its track, near Soire le Château, while commanded by his son, Capt. Bruneau. (Author's collection)

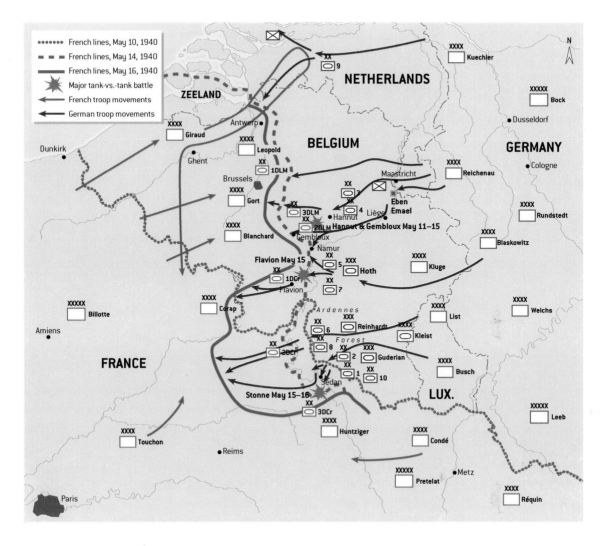

Map labels:

French lines, May 10, 1940
French lines, May 14, 1940
French lines, May 16, 1940
Major tank-vs.-tank battle
French troop movements
German troop movements

NETHERLANDS
ZEELAND
BELGIUM
GERMANY
FRANCE
LUX.

Dunkirk
Antwerp
Ghent
Brussels
Dusseldorf
Cologne
Maastricht
Liège
Eben Emael
Hannut
Gembloux
Namur
Ardennes
Flavion
Forest
Sedan
Amiens
Flavion May 15
Stonne May 15–16
Reims
Paris
Metz

Hannut & Gembloux May 11–15

XXXX Kuechler
XXXXX Bock
XXXX Reichenau
XXXX Rundstedt
XXXX Blaskowitz
XXXX Kluge
XXXX Weichs
XXXX List
XXXXX Kleist
XXXX Guderian
XXXX Busch
XXXXX Leeb
XXXXX Pretelat
XXXX Réquin
XXXX Condé
XXXX Huntziger
XXXX Touchon
XXXXX Billotte
XXXX Corap
XXXX Blanchard
XXXX Gort
XXXX Leopold
XXXX Giraud

XX 9
XX 3
XX 4
1DLM
3DLM
2DLM
XX 5
Hoth
XX 7
1DCr
XX 6
Reinhardt
XX 8
XX 2
XX 1
10
2DCr
3DCr

N

At first, Manstein's plan fell on deaf ears. As in France, the most senior German commanders viewed the Ardennes as an impenetrable tangle of hills and forest. Three factors shifted the balance in favor of Manstein's gamble. On a routine flight in bad weather in January 1940, a Luftwaffe officer carrying portions of the Luftwaffe plan for the invasion landed in Belgium. Although the officer managed to destroy most of the maps, there was concern in Berlin that the original plan had been compromised. The conservative nature of the original plan did not appeal to Hitler, and he expressed some vague thoughts about a bolder scheme towards Sedan, the site of the great 1870 German victory. Military aides, sympathetic to Manstein, connived to arrange a meeting between Hitler and Manstein where his Ardennes plan could be explained. Gen. Franz Halder, Chief of the Army's General Staff, had originally opposed Manstein's scheme, but after a series of wargames and staff studies in the autumn and early winter of 1939–40, he began to appreciate that such a gamble was Germany's only way to win a quick and decisive victory against the French and avoid another protracted war akin to 1914–18.

Panzer Breakthrough at Sedan: May 10–16, 1940

The 4.Panzer Division was part of the "matador's red cape" with Army Group B attacking through the Netherlands and Belgium. This is one of its PzKpfw IV Ausf. D, evident from the division's "crow's foot" insignia on the glacis plate. (NARA)

This confluence of forces led to Manstein's scheme being adopted as the basis for the final version of *Fall Gelb* (Case Yellow), the German codename for the attack on France and the Low Countries. The "red cape" role would be played by Army Group B, primarily an infantry force of 29 divisions that would sweep across the Dutch frontier heading for Belgium. The bull-fighter's sword would be Gerd von Rundstedt's Army Group A which contained seven of the Army's ten panzer divisions. These were concentrated in four corps, but the most critical role would be played by von Kleist's Panzer Group which contained Guderian's XIX Armee Korps (XIX.AK) and Wietersheim's XIV.AK which intended to cross the Meuse at Sedan.

The German Army launched its attack on May 10, 1940, adding to the matador's distraction with dramatic flourishes including an airborne assault on the Belgian fortress at Eban-Emael. The Allies responded as the German plan had anticipated; four Allied field armies marched into Belgium and into the trap. Army Group A's panzer spearheads began their advance through Luxembourg, attracting little attention. Its pace was imperiled more by traffic jams than by Allied counteraction. On schedule, the German troops appeared at the Meuse on May 13, and after a spectacular Luftwaffe bombardment, German infantry began the river crossings. By the following day, elements of four panzer divisions were over the Meuse and the hapless French reservists in this neglected sector were routed.

Guderian was especially pleased by the performance of his corps. However, one of his greatest anxieties was the presence of the Mont-Dieu plateau south of the Meuse crossing sites which could threaten the bridgehead if occupied by French troops. Guderian expected that sooner or later, the French would stage a counterattack towards Sedan from Mont-Dieu, and indeed such an operation was already underway. To shield the vital Meuse bridgehead while Guderian's panzers raced westward, 10.Panzer Division was assigned the task of seizing and holding the Mont-Dieu plateau. The fighting for Stonne on Mont-Dieu is the setting for the duel between the PzKpfw IV and Char B1 bis in one of the most violent battles of the 1940 campaign.

COMBAT: DUEL AT STONNE

A German officer later recalled: "There are three battles I can never forget: Stonne, Stalingrad, and Monte Cassino." While the latter two battles are well known in English-language histories of World War II, Stonne remains obscure. Most German accounts call it "the Verdun of 1940"; the town changed hands 17 times in two days of intense fighting on May 15–16. Stonne sat on the crest of the Mont-Dieu

The first French counterattack against the Sedan bridgehead was conducted by the reservist 55e DI. Its 213e Régiment d'Infanterie was supported by the 7e BCL equipped with the FCM-36 infantry tank, with one tank company assigned to each infantry battalion. Although the FCM-36 proved very resistant to German 37mm anti-tank guns, by the afternoon of May 14, the 7e BCL had lost 29 of its 39 FCM tanks around Bulson. This is "Le Mistral" with the village of Maisoncelle evident in the background. (NARA)

(God's Mountain) plateau about 15km (nine miles) south of Sedan. Its highpoint, on the eastern side of the town, was called Pain de Sucre (Sugar Loaf). The Germans wanted control of Stonne to shield the Sedan bridgeheads and the French Army needed it as the springboard to attack the Meuse bridgeheads. Fighting in the foreground of Stonne took place on May 14 when the 55e Division d'Infanterie attempted to counterattack the German bridgehead with the support of the FCM-36 light tanks of the 4e and 7e BCC. These attacks were crushed and the French reservists were routed.

Guderian selected the 10.Panzer Division to seize Mont-Dieu because it had been the last of the three panzer divisions in Panzergruppe Kliest to arrive at the Meuse. Since the mission was primarily defensive, Infanterie-Regiment Großdeutschland (IRGD) was added to provide a firmer defensive base. In the meantime, the commander of the French 2e Armée, Gen. Charles Hutzinger, had assigned the task of counterattacking the Sedan bridgehead to Gen. J. Flavigny's 21e Corps d'Armée. Flavigny was one of the French Army's tank experts. When he went forward that afternoon, he encountered officers from the routed 213e Régiment d'Infanterie who had been part of the first Sedan counterattack. This panic-stricken officers warned of hundreds of German tanks swarming across the Meuse. Flavigny's orders from Huntzinger were to establish a defensive reserve position to block the roads from Mont-Dieu southwest towards Paris and to attack "with the most brutal energy and with complete disregard of casualties" towards Sedan. He was allotted the 3e DCr and the 3e DIM (Division d'Infanterie Motorisée), but they were still on the road and did not begin arriving until May 14. Huntzinger's orders were ambiguous. What was the priority? The defensive mission to block any German advance

The standard French infantry anti-tank gun was the Hotchkiss 25mm modèle 1934, and there were 4,400 in service in May 1940. It was capable of penetrating the thin armor of German panzers at normal combat ranges. (Author's collection)

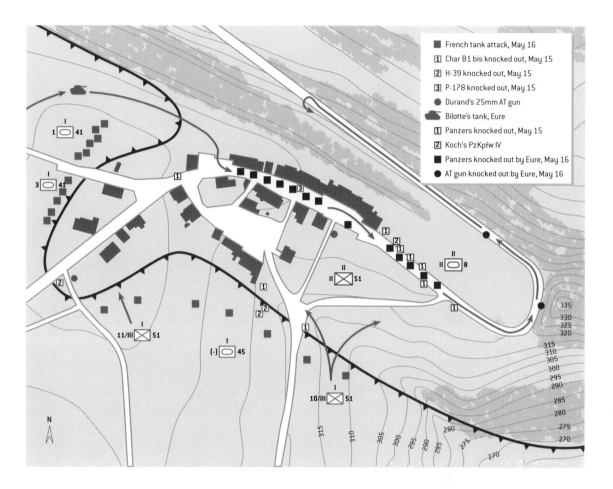

Legend:
- French tank attack, May 16
- [1] Char B1 bis knocked out, May 15
- [2] H-39 knocked out, May 15
- [3] P-178 knocked out, May 15
- Durand's 25mm AT gun
- Bilotte's tank, Eure
- [1] Panzers knocked out, May 15
- [2] Koch's PzKpfw IV
- Panzers knocked out by Eure, May 16
- AT gun knocked out by Eure, May 16

Billotte's Rampage in Stonne, May 16, 1940.

southwards or the counteroffensive to smash the German bridgehead at Sedan? Were the two missions to be staged concurrently, or were they be staged successively?

The 3e DCr had been ordered forward from Reims starting on the afternoon of May 12 and arrived at Le Chesne on the Ardennes canal, 10km southwest of Stonne, early on the morning of May 14. The divisional commander originally thought they merely were being moved to another training ground. The 60–90km trip had been slowed by extensive bomb damage in the towns enroute as well as by roads clogged with fleeing refugees. The two Char B1 bis battalions, the 41e and 49e BCC, had a combined total of 63 tanks at Reims, instead of the usual 69, and departed with 62 tanks. The two light tank battalions were also understrength as one company of Hotchkiss H-39 tanks had been sent off to Norway to support the Allied expeditionary force there. The division lacked refueling vehicles, divisional engineer and anti-tank units.

When the 3e DCr finally reached the Mont-Dieu area, the division's Char B1 bis force was depleted and had only 53 Char B1 bis in operational condition at the end of May 14, mainly due to mechanical breakdowns connected with the Naeder steering system. The division began the laborious task of refueling its tanks after the road-march and so was not ready until the afternoon of May 14. The 3e DIM was behind the tank columns and began to arrive late on May 14.

This is a view from inside Stonne looking east along the road where the initial German tank attack took place. Two of the tank wrecks are evident in the background, but this photo was taken on July 19, over a month after the battle, and the tanks had presumably been moved off the road. (NARA)

When pressed by Flavigny about when his division would be ready to attack Sedan, the 3e DCr commander, Gén. Antoine Brocard, suggested May 15 would be best since after the refueling was complete, it would take two to three hours to move his units the 15km from Le Chesne to the Bois-de-Mont-Dieu, and then another two to three hours to refuel again in order to reach Sedan, meaning that the 3e DCr would not be ready to attack Sedan until that evening. As mentioned earlier, Flavigny had witnessed the poor performance of the better-trained 2e DCr a week before on exercise, and was even more skeptical of the ability of the incomplete 3e DCr to carry out an offensive mission. As a result, Flavigny followed the defensive intent of Huntzinger's orders and ignored its offensive mission. He ordered the 3e DCr to set up *bouchons* (corks) composed of a Char B1 bis and H-39 light tanks at the crossings over the Ardennes canal south of Mont-Dieu.

The first combat unit to deploy into the village of Stonne was from the 6e GRDI (Groupe de reconnaissance d'Infanterie) which was the divisional reconnaissance element of the 3e DIM. The unit had split into smaller sections to conduct its mission along a wide front; Groupe Est (East Group) entered Stonne early on May 14 and included a pair of Panhard 178 armored cars. One its main tasks was to discover what was happening with the first wave of the attack being staged by the 55e DI. The armored cavalry scouts ran into fleeing soldiers from the 55e DI and it was soon apparent that the initial counterattack had failed. The 6e GRDI scouts were followed by the I/67e RI (1re Battalion, 67e Régiment d'Infanterie of the 3e DIM) which took up defensive positions in the town. They were supported by a pair of 25mm anti-tank guns, and a single 47mm anti-tank gun from the divisional anti-tank company.

On the German side, the lead element of the advance on Stonne was the Großdeutschland Regiment which had headed south of the Meuse bridgehead in advance of the 10.Panzer Division. In the early morning hours of May 15, the

Großdeutschland Regiment was advancing on a broad front with I./IRGD moving directly towards Stonne with II./IRGD to the east near Pain de Sucre and the Sturmpioniere-Batallion.43 to the west of the town. A lead tank column from II./Pz.Rgt.8, consisting of six PzKpfw IV tanks and five light tanks, moved up the narrow hair-pin road on the north side of the town. After a short artillery preparation, the German attack on the town began around 0500 hours on May 15, with the five PzKpfw IV leading the attack by swinging around the hair-pin turn on the east side of the town, moving towards the town's main street.

The nearest French 25mm gun was commanded by a veteran of the International Brigades in the Spanish Civil War, Sgt. Durand, and he waited until the lead PzKpfw IV was only a few dozen meters away before opening fire. At the head of the column was the PzKpfw IV, number 700, of Hptm. Ottens, the company commander of 7./Pz.Rgt.8. At such a close range, the 25mm had no difficulty penetrating the PzKpfw IV's frontal armor, and after the first hit, Durand's crew fired several more shots to make sure the tank had been knocked out. They next turned to the second PzKpfw IV in the column, number 711, and the round struck the side driver's visor, decapitating the driver and stunning the radioman. The devastation in the driver's compartment prompted the turret crew to abandon the tank, and when they later returned, they found that the radioman had later been killed by rifle fire when attempting to escape the tank. The third PzKpfw IV by now was blocked by the other two and hit by the 25mm gun; an internal fire erupted and the tank exploded in a

This was the lead tank of the German column, number 700, the company command tank of Hptm. Ottens which was knocked out by 25mm fire. (NARA)

PREVIOUS PAGES:
Capt. Billotte's Char B1 bis "Eure" swung to the left flank of the 1e Compagnie, 41e BCC attack and entered the town of Stonne on the main street near the village church. A column of Pz.Rgt.8 tanks was lined up preparing for a counterattack, and were taking shelter along the buildings on the street. The column consisted mainly of PzKpfw II light tanks, escorted by a few PzKpfw III and PzKpfw IV tanks for support. Billotte instructed his driver, Sgt. Durupt, to engage the lead tank at point-blank range with the 75mm gun while he fired at the trailing tank. The panzer column was so closely bunched together that once the first and last tanks were hit, the others tanks could not move. Billotte proceeded down the street, systematically engaging and knocking out every tank in the column. After exiting the village, Billotte encountered a trailing column of tanks advancing down the road and destroyed these as well. The Germans fought back, but their guns could not penetrate the heavy frontal armor of the Char B1 bis; Billotte's tank was struck 140 times in a few minutes of combat. Exiting the town, Billotte directed his tank down the hairpin turn towards the valley below, destroying two 37mm anti-tank guns in the process. He finally turned back and returned back through the village. In total, Billotte claimed 13 German tanks, though the number may be a bit high due to the presence of several wrecked tanks including Koch's PzKpfw IV from the previous day's fighting.

catastrophic detonation which set off the ammunition and fuel and blew the tank apart. Durand's crew then hitched up the gun to their Renault UE tractor and repositioned further west. By this stage, the German infantry had entered the village and a few PzKpfw II light tanks passed the disabled PzKpfw IV and attempted to fight their way into the town. A mêlée broke out with three of the PzKpfw II being hit by the 25mm guns, but both Panhard 178 armored cars were disabled during the fighting. One of the PzKpfw II managed to fight its way through the town and exit on the west side, only to be hit by the other 25mm gun of Lt. Salaberry of the 6e GRDI. Nevertheless, the vigorous attack by the light tanks had thrown the balance in favor of the German attacks, and the I/67e RI withdrew south out of the town. By this stage, the surviving three PzKpfw IV had fought their way through town to the south and took up positions there.

Senior French commanders had expected Flavigny to attack the Sedan bridgehead and instead learned that his corps was trapped in a defensive battle short of the objective. The Commander-in-Chief of the northeast front, Gen. Alphonse Georges, blasted Huntzinger. The previous day, May 14, Huntzinger's HQ was distracted while moving, and it took until 0800 on May 15 before he telephoned Flavigny and ordered him to stage the counterattack on the Sedan bridgehead with the 3e DCr and 3e DIM that day. Flavigny's two divisional commanders arrived at his command post at 1000, and he instructed them to start the attack by 1400. It became apparent that it was much easier to scatter the 3e DCr tanks all over the countryside than to reform them into coherent units. Brocard reported that he had only 41 Char B1 bis for the attack due to problems bringing the others back from the Ardennes canal defenses; by noon the total had been reduced to 34 due to combat losses in Stonne. Flavigny was so dismayed by Brocard's lack of enthusiasm that he assigned the 3e DIM commander,

Gen. Paul Bertin-Boussu, to take overall command of both divisions. Instead of a coordinated attack, Flavigny's corps would spend most of the day trying to concentrate their forces for the counterattack, while at the same time being distracted by the need to keep dispatching troops and tanks to prevent the Germans from breaking out of Stonne.

The 67e RI set up anti-tank positions south of the town and 13 Hotchkiss H-39 tanks of the 1/45e BCC arrived to stage an immediate counterattack. While advancing towards the town, they were taken under fire from PzKpfw IV, number 711; after having been disabled by 25mm fire during the initial attack, the surviving turret crew of number 711 re-boarded the tank and took the French tanks under fire at a range of 600 meters. They struck two of the H-39, putting them out of action. A platoon under Lt. Chambert continued the attack into the town, coming under fire from the 37mm anti-tank guns of Panzer-Jäger Kompanie.14, but they managed to knock out two German tanks in a close-range duel. Although they managed to push into the town, the light tanks lacked infantry support and were eventually forced to withdraw. The next French unit to attack was the 3/49e BCC with three Char B1 bis tanks under Lt. Paul Caravéo, which began moving towards the town around 0730 hours. The appearance of the three monstrous tanks on the southern edge of the town prompted the German infantry to temporarily withdraw, but once again, with no infantry support, the three tanks couldn't possibly hold the town so they took up positions on the southwest outskirts. Around 0940 hours, Caravéo's tanks noticed Oberfeldwebel Hans Hindeland's anti-tank section trying to deploy three 37mm anti-tank guns at the western entrance to the town. The Char B1 bis company began to move forward, firing machine guns. The German gunners opened fire at close range but were horrified to see the tracers at the base of their anti-tank projectiles bounce upward when they failed to penetrate. One of the guns was destroyed at a range of only 100 meters and

OPPOSITE:
This is the PzKpfw IV Ausf. D number 711, which was the second tank in the German column and was knocked out by 25mm fire. Tank number 700 can be seen to the west closer to the village. This photo was taken on July 19, 1940, and presumably 711 had been pushed off the road during the clean-up. (NARA)

This close-up of number 711 shows numerous hits and gouges from 25mm gun fire and other sources, including the direct hit on the driver's visor that killed the driver and stunned the radio operator. (NARA)

a second gun had several of its crew wounded. The intact gun, commanded by Feldwebel Giesemann, noticed a ribbed surface on the left side of a Char B1 bis – S/Lt. Yves Rohou's Char B1 bis "Chinon" – and hoped it might be a vulnerable point. A single hit on the grill caused fire to spurt out of the side of the tank. The Char B1 bis further to the east were taken under fire by PzKpfw IV, No. 711. The tank's gunner, Feldwebel Karl Koch, later recalled: "Between engagements, we were looking for ammunition from the (knocked out) panzers in front of us. After a while, a fourth tank appeared through the orchard. It was a real monster and we had no idea that France had tanks like that. We fired 20 shots at it without success. However, after a few more shots, we managed to knock off its track. After a while, a fifth tank appears, another B1 firing all its weapons. But it had not spotted us. We fired, but could not knock it out until a ricochet hit the turret. The next shot hit it in the rear. Calm returned and we abandoned our tank again because we had exhausted the ammunition." Koch had hit "Hautvillers", jamming the turret and knocking off the tracks on one side. The crew abandoned the tank and were captured. His other victim was "Gaillac" which eventually exploded, killing the whole crew.

The next French action was the first coordinated tank-infantry attack involving a few H-39 from the 45e BCC, a few FCM-36 from the 4e BCC, three remaining Char B1 bis of Caravéo's 3/49e BCC, the I/67e RI and a company from the newly arrived I/51e RI. The German infantry took a heavy pounding from French 155mm artillery fire in advance of the infantry attack which started around 1040. The I/51e RI company attacked on the western side of town, and the remainder of the force attacked towards the northeast. About 500 meters from Stonne, the Char B1 bis tanks halted to provide over-watch, firing their 75mm guns in support while the smaller Hotchkiss and FCM tanks accompanied the infantry into the town. The French infantry, with tank support, again regained the town and around 1100 the surviving

The third PzKpfw IV in the column suffered a catastrophic ammunition and fuel fire that blew the tank apart. The turret can be seen some distance away towards the village. (NARA)

Großdeutschland infantrymen were authorized to withdraw back towards the original start point near the regimental HQ. By this stage, Panzer-Jäger Kompagnie.14 had suffered 28 casualties, and lost 12 vehicles and six 37mm anti-tank guns. French losses to this point were three Char B1 bis plus at least five damaged, and two H-39 lost and three damaged. Four Char B1 bis had their 47mm turret guns disabled when high-explosive projectiles prematurely detonated in the gun tube.

After the French infantry took up positions in Stonne, the tanks pulled off the hill to replenish and repair. The Luftwaffe staged a Ju-87 Stuka attack on the town and this was followed by a heavy artillery bombardment. The artillery fire was so heavy that the French infantry pulled out of the village again, but the Germans were in no position to re-occupy the ruins. Around 1530, once the fire had died down, the French infantry returned to the town, accompanied by Caravéo's Char B1 bis tanks.

The 10.Panzer Division commander, Generalleutnant Ferdinand Schaal, ordered another attack on the town at 1500, but the Großdeutschland commander pointed out that his unit had been on the march for days, had been fighting continuously over the past few days, and were thoroughly exhausted. The German attack was delayed until 1800 and was conducted with fresh infantry from I./Schützen-Regiment.69. The evening attack pushed the French out of the center of town but the French infantry continued to cling to the southern edge of town at nightfall and the center of town remained a no-man's land for most of the night.

Flavigny had planned to conduct the counterattack towards Sedan by 1400 hours, but Brocard reported that he could only have eight Char B1 bis ready by 1500 hours, as the others were either caught up in the fighting in Stonne, not yet fueled, or hadn't arrived. Flavigny then postponed the attack towards Sedan until 1730, and he ordered Brocard to lead with the available Hotchkiss H-39 tanks. One of the Char B1 bis companies did not learn of the postponement and headed off on its own, only to run into German anti-tank gun positions where it lost two tanks. By early evening, the

3e DCr only had only 29 Char B1 bis tanks available and the plans for a major counterattack on the Sedan bridgehead simply petered out.

Gen. Bertin-Bossu decided to stage an early morning attack to secure Stonne. During the night of May 15–16, the fresh 41e BCC moved two of its companies near the town to prepare for an early morning counterattack. This consisted of the seven Char B1 bis tanks under Capt. Billotte of 1/41e BCC and seven Char B1 bis tanks under Capt. Delepierre of 3/41e BCC. The attacking infantry force was the III/51e RI and they were directly supported by H-39 light tanks of the 45e BCC. The attack began around 0430 hours on May 16 with a 45-minute artillery bombardment. The first wave of Char B1 bis tanks arrived outside Stonne at around 0515 and advanced

One of Koch's victims during the fighting was Char B1 bis No. 416 "Hautvillers" of 3/49e BCC which took several hits through the engine grating. The crew, led by Sous lieutenant Jacques Klein, escaped the tank before it blew up and they were captured. (NARA)

This close-up of the radiator air intake grill on "Hautvillers" shows how two rounds from Koch's 75mm gun managed to penetrate into the engine compartment, setting the tank on fire. (NARA)

to within 100 meters of the western side of town while engaging several anti-tank guns and tanks. Billotte headed directly into the town, shooting up a column of 13 panzers, as is recounted in more detail here with the associated illustration.

During the attack, one Char B1 bis overturned in a gully, two more Char B1 bis broke down, and one was missing in action. In the meantime, the III/51e RI had closed on the town under the cover of the Hotchkiss light tanks and after nearly an hour of skirmishing, controlled Stonne again by 0700 hours. The Germans contested the latest attack with a heavy artillery bombardment at around 1000 hours, followed by a Stuka attack and another round of artillery shelling. German attacks on either side of Stonne in the morning and early afternoon were broken up by the French infantry. By late afternoon, the 51e RI had taken so many casualties as a result of continuous artillery fire that they pulled back to the edge of town. When the German infantry tried to reoccupy the town around 1430 hours, the French counterattacked and threw them out again; the Germans counterattacked around 1630 hours, but within a half-hour had been pushed out again by the 51e RI. The Germans attempted to reinforce Stonne with troops from Schützen-Regiment.64, but one platoon was spotted by Lt. Doumercq's Char B1 bis "Riquewihr" which charged them, running over some of the infantry in the process. Doumercq was dubbed "the butcher of Stonne" after this horrifying attack. The final German attack around 1745 hours pushed the French out for the last time.

The tank fighting for Stonne petered out after the evening of May 16. The 10.Panzer Division was pulled out and replaced by two infantry divisions; likewise the Char B1 bis battalions were withdrawn for actions in other sectors. Casualties in the Großdeutschland Regiment alone for the two days of fighting were 570 including 103 killed, more than half its casualties during the whole France campaign. French casualties were equally severe, particularly in the two infantry regiments taking part. Tank casualties were about 25 panzers and 33 French tanks. The fighting continued around Stonne for more than a week, but both sides substituted infantry forces for this brutal slogging match. The fighting for Stonne was often called the "Verdun of 1940", more for the later stages of the battle when entrenched infantry were subjected to relentless artillery barrages. The two Char B1 bis battalions of the 3e DCr continued in action in the ensuing weeks of the campaign, but in a piecemeal fashion.

THE OTHER CHAR B1 BIS UNITS

The combat fate of the other Char B1 bis battalions were depressingly similar. All three of the divisions were inexperienced which was very evident from the problems they had in simply moving to the battle-zone and remaining ready for combat. The road-marches invariably left some Char B1 bis behind with mechanical problems, and the units were often tied up for hours trying to get the support vehicles to join the tanks to begin the laborious refueling process.

Gén. Marie Bruneau's 1e DCr was intended to take part in the original lunge into Belgium, but remained behind as a potential counterattack reserve. Movement was delayed by refugees on the roads and disrupted by the usual dithering in the French high command over its mission. In a parallel of the mission of the 3e DCr, it was dispatched to the 9e Armée to deal with the threat posed by the other German Meuse bridgehead near Dinant by Hoth's XV.AK which included Rommel's 7.Panzer Division and the 5.Panzer Division. In the early morning hours of May 15, the 28e and 37e BCC had reached Flavion, but their Char B1 bis tanks were nearly out of fuel and the divisional fuel trucks were stuck in traffic jams; lack of fuel meant that the engines were off and low battery power impeded radio communication. In this impaired state, the 1e DCR was repeatedly engaged by elements of both of Hoth's panzer divisions in a swirling series of close-range tank battles. After violent initial contact, Rommel's 7.Panzer Division was ordered to skirt around the French tank concentrations and head deep behind French lines towards Philippeville. The 28e BCC was caught during refueling and through the course of the day lost 23 tanks despite exacting a heavy price on the 5.Panzer Division. The 37e BCC staged a number of counterattacks but lost 21 tanks, most often in engagements with German 105mm field guns. German losses were around 60 panzers, mainly in 5.Panzer Division. The 1e DCr was decimated in the battle of Flavion by superior tactics rather than superior equipment. The 5.Panzer Division had only 32 PzKpfw IV compared to more than double that number of Char B1 bis, but the German battalion commanders skillfully used their radios to maneuver their out-gunned companies and destroy the French tank companies in a piecemeal fashion. The panzer crews were shocked to see their 37mm and 75mm rounds bounce off the Char B1 bis, but by the afternoon the division had moved its artillery forward for improvised use in the direct fire role, successfully beating back a number of attacks by the 37e BCC. The 1e DCr was no longer combat effective after the battle at Flavion, and was gradually annihilated in a series of small skirmishes over the next few weeks; Gen. Bruneau, and part of the headquarters, was captured on May 18.

While the 1e DCr fought valiantly but ineffectively at Flavion, the 2e DCr was frittered away. The division was ordered to move towards Charleroi behind the 1e DCr, but the rail movement was disrupted by German air attacks and the chaos in Belgium. When finally de-trained and assigned to establish a defensive line, the division was scattered over a 70km front-line with little central control. Part of its division artillery was overrun and the division split in half by the German panzer advances; it was eventually given orders to cork up the Oise river crossings, scattering its tank battalions in small-scale engagements. The division's Char B1 bis saw numerous engagements during this period, but seldom larger than platoon-sized actions. On May 19, attempts were made to consolidate its scattered elements, but by this stage only about 20 Char B1 bis were still under divisional control. The reconstituted division was squandered again in a series of futile maneuvers south of Amiens, finally taking part in the battle at Abbeville in early June with a number of other armored units including elements of de Gaulle's improvised 4e DCr.

In contrast to the immature DCr, the cavalry's DLM proved much more combat-effective, most notably in the battles fought by Prioux's cavalry corps at Hannut and the subsequent skirmishing on the approaches to the Gembloux gap on May 11–16. While this might be attributed in part to a better organization structure, these divisions enjoyed a longer period of development and training as well as a clearer doctrinal mission that more closely matched their actual combat assignment.

The 1e DCR was shot up in a series of battles around Flavion on May 15. This is "Poitou II" (no. 451), of Capt. Jacques Lehoux who commanded 3/37e BCC. This tank, along with "Nivernais II," attacked the advancing 8.Infanterie Division near Denée but were taken under fire by 105mm field guns and 88mm Flak. This tank took a direct hit on the turret leading to an ammunition fire which killed the entire crew. (NARA)

STATISTICS AND ANALYSIS

The combat actions of the Char B1 bis in 1940 are in many ways reminiscent of the surprise debuts of other heavy tanks later in the war where the tank's armor made them nearly impervious to anti-tank weapons. There are numerous accounts of "tank panic" among the German infantry in the Soviet Union, during Operation *Barbarossa* in 1941, after encounters with the KV heavy tank. As with the Char B1 bis in 1940, these skirmishes often caused local difficulties, and, as was the case in France in 1940, the broader problems afflicting the Red Army meant that small technological

Many of the Char B1 bis from the later production batches that were not incorporated into the armored divisions were assigned to ad-hoc independent companies that saw combat in June 1940. This is "Ney" (no. 530) of the 348e CACC which was knocked out on the morning of June 4, 1940, after running over a mine during the battle of Abbeville. (MHI)

advantages could do little to redress the tactical or operational balance. Billotte's rampage through Stonne is reminiscent of Michael Wittman's rampage with his Tiger tank at Villers-Bocage in Normandy in 1944, though the later action had more significant tactical results than Billotte's.

The combat record of the Char B1 bis in 1940 presents a very mixed picture. On the one hand, many individual Char B1 bis tanks performed exceptionally well in small actions due to their impressive armor. The 10.Panzer Division war-diary records encounters with 60-ton "super-heavy tanks," greatly exaggerating their actual size and power. The central problem facing the Char B1 bis was their incorporation into armored divisions which were inadequately prepared and ill-used by higher commands.

According to a postwar French Army study, overall French tank losses in 1940 amounted to 1,749 tanks lost out of 4,071 engaged, of which 1,669 were lost to gunfire, 45 to mines and 35 to aircraft. This amounts to about 43 percent of the deployed force compared to German losses of about 35 percent. However, the French losses were substantially amplified by the large numbers of tanks that were abandoned or scuttled by their own crews.

In total, about 370 Char B1 and B1 bis tanks took part in the fighting. Precise figures are difficult to determine since small numbers of tanks continued to dribble into action in the final weeks of the campaign in small ad hoc formations. Some records exist for about 300 of these tanks, so it is possible to make some rough assessments of the causes of Char B1 bis casualties. Char B1 bis tank losses appear to have been evenly divided between direct combat losses and indirect combat losses. The direct combat losses were due primarily to the Germans' improvised use of heavy artillery, with the vast majority due to 105mm field guns and 88mm Flak guns which were the only weapons that could reliably penetrate the Char B1 bis' heavy armor. Losses to German tank and anti-tank guns were very few – from incomplete French

The Char B1 bis remained in combat through much of the war in German service. This example was used for beach defense in the Dieppe area where it was captured by Canadian troops in the summer of 1944. Some Char B1 bis tanks recaptured from the Germans were turned over to Free French units and saw combat in 1945 in the reduction of the German garrisons in the isolated Atlantic coast ports. (NAC PA143908)

accounts probably under two dozen. At least six Char B1 bis were lost to mines, at least two to air attacks, and at least four to fratricide including French anti-tank and tank guns. Indirect combat losses consisted mainly of mechanical breakdowns or fuel exhaustion followed by crew abandonment. At least 60 Char B1 bis were deliberately scuttled by their crews due to damage, encirclement, or other factors; scuttling of tanks became very common in the final weeks of the campaign. A number of tanks were lost due to accidents such as overturning or running into swamps or soft ground. There were several recurring sources of mechanical breakdowns, with the delicate Naeder steering system being the chief culprit. Other common sources of mechanical breakdowns included engine failures, transmission failures, and engine fires. Many tanks were abandoned due to multiple problems, often including a combination of battle damage and mechanical problems. Although some historical accounts suggest that fuel exhaustion was a primary cause of Char B1 bis loss, evidence for this is lacking. At least 18 Char B1 bis tanks were damaged or suffered breakdowns during the campaign but were recovered and transported back to repair bases; only a handful of Char B1 bis tanks were still operational at the end of the campaign. After the war, the German Army recovered damaged tanks for re-use and by October 1940 had accumulated 161 Char B1 bis; in March 1943, the Wehrmacht had 125 Char B1 bis tanks operational in all theaters.

Char B1 Bis Tank Casualties 1940					
Unit	Division (DCr)	Combat losses	Abandoned/ Scuttled	Recovered/ Intact	Unknown
8e BCC	2e	17	16	1	2
15e BCC	2e	13	17	2	0
28e BCC	1e	20	30	2	17
37e BCC	1e	18	14	0	5
41e BCC	3e	15	17	2	1
46e BCC	4e	10	19	3	5
47e BCC	4e	7	8	9	10
49e BCC	3e	16	4	1	13
Sep. Companies	n/a	12	14	1	26
Total		128	139	21	79

The 15e BCC provides a typical example of a unit's fate in the campaign. Of its 32 Char B1 bis tanks at the start of the campaign, 11 suffered mechanical failures, 11 were knocked out in combat primarily by artillery and tank fire, 2 were lost to mines, 4 were destroyed by their own crews, 2 were abandoned or surrendered, and only 2 survived the campaign intact. In the case of the mechanical failures, in most cases the crew destroyed the vehicle.

The PzKpfw IV was not a star performer in France, but an excellent supporting player in a superior team. Photos in this book document PzKpfw IVs in action in late June 1940 after having driven through the Ardennes, fought in numerous skirmishes up to the Channel coast, and then advanced through the depths of eastern France to Alsace, an amazing display of durability by 1940 standards. The armor protection on the PzKpfw IV was not adequate against even the lightest French anti-tank guns, and the PzKpfw IV showed an alarming tendency towards catastrophic ammunition and fuel fires. Nevertheless, the PzKpfw IV had considerable growth potential due to its prudent design, and the armor weakness could be addressed with upgrades. The PzKpfw IV did not perform especially well in tank-vs.-tank fighting, but it had never been designed for that role. It remained armed with a short 75mm gun until the tank panic of 1941 when the Wehrmacht was confronted with the well-armed and well-armored T-34 and KV tanks. A long, high-velocity 75mm tank gun was required to deal with these, and the smaller turret ring of the PzKpfw III was not adequate to handle to recoil forces of this new 75mm KwK40 gun. As a result, the role of the PzKpfw IV changed, no longer being a fire-support tank for the PzKpfw III battle tank. Instead, the PzKpfw IV with the long 75mm KwK40 gun replaced the PzKpfw III as the backbone of the panzer divisions. It's worth noting that the German Army could have initiated this shift a year earlier, as encounters with the heavily armored French tanks such as the Char B1 bis as well as British tanks such as the Matilda provided evidence of a shift towards more heavily armored tanks. However, in 1940–41 the Wehrmacht did not place as much importance on technological advantages on the battlefield as it did on tank reliability, crew training, and effective doctrine. The quest for technological perfection often led to tanks with excellent performance on paper, but heavier armor often came at the expense of reliability and durability. The Wehrmacht attitude to this issue changed after 1941, and this controversy was echoed in 1944–45 over the combat performance of the Sherman tank versus the heavily armored Panther tank, but with the Allied/Axis polarities reversed from those of 1940.

The Panzerwaffe suffered heavy losses in the France campaign, though not as severe as those of the French Army. After two weeks of fighting, Panzergruppe Kliest had only half its tanks operational, with about 30 percent knocked out in combat or suffering serious mechanical breakdowns and another 20 percent temporarily unavailable due to short-term mechanical or other problems. Of the 2,439 panzers originally committed 822, or about 34 percent, were total losses after five weeks of fighting. In the case of the PzKpfw IV, the percentage was almost identical, 97 tanks expended of the 278 originally committed. Casualties were heaviest in the initial fighting in May, with 77 PzKpfw IV lost compared to only 20 in June. Detailed figures for the number of mechanical breakdowns are not available and are not as relevant as in the French case, since, as the victors, the Wehrmacht could recover damaged or broken-down tanks and put them back into service. The next year, these same PzKpfw IV Ausf. D would see combat again in Russia and North Africa.

After the encounters with Soviet T-34 and KV tanks in 1941, the PzKpfw IV was steadily up-gunned and its armor thickened. By 1943, it was hardly recognizable from the versions that had served in France in 1940. (NARA)

FURTHER READING

My interest in the 1940 France campaign was inspired by reading Alistair Horne's classic *To Lose a Battle* when it appeared in 1969. Since then, much more has been written about the campaign, but the Horne book has stood the test of time and remains an enlightening and accessible account. From the German perspective, the recent Freiser book provides a provocative look at many of the key tactical and operational controversies. From the French perspective, the two Doughty books are essential reading. The Kiesling study helps explain some the deeper causes of the French problems while Saint-Martin covers the specifics of the French armored force.

There has been an upsurge in writing on the tanks of 1940, especially from the French side. François Vauvillier has rejuvenated the old *Histoire et Guerre* magazine which was renamed as *Guerre, Blindés & Materiél* and it has become the premier venue for new research on French Army mechanization and the 1940 campaign. A number of small technical monographs on the Char B1 bis have appeared, but no doubt the most impressive reference is Bonnaud's superb study which details the first Char B1 bis unit, the 15e BCC, down to the fate of each individual tank; Bonnaud's father served in the unit. The battle of Stonne is extremely well covered from the French side, especially in the special issue of *Batailles* magazine by Eric Denis, and the new Autant book.

Dennis Showalter's recent book on the panzers is a fine example of popular history, offering considerable insight into the origins of the German panzer force prior to 1940. This subject has been covered in depth by a number of academic studies; the Habeck account offers an intriguing look at the often-ignored synergy between Soviet and German developments. In spite of the tremendous amount of ink spilled on the technical aspects of German panzers in recent years, the coverage of the early development of the PzKpfw IV remains spotty.

Besides these published source, I used a variety of archival sources. The National Archives and Records Administration in College Park, Maryland, has copies of the KTB (Kriegstagebuch: War diaries) of Guderian's XIX.AK which helps provide the background for the combat actions described here. The KTB for the 10.Panzer Division was badly damaged by fire at the Heeresarchiv Potsdam in February 1942, so it is less useful though bits remain. I also used the records of the Waffenamt of the OKH (Oberkommando des Heeres) at NARA for data on German tank production and losses.

David Lehmann and Dr. Dirk Rottgardt were kind enough to provide me with extensive French documentation on tank strength and tank production as well as their own writings on the subject, much of them unpublished. In 1947, the French Assemblée Nationale established a commission to inquire into the events of the 1940 campaign, and the multi-volume "Rapport fait au nom de la Commission chargée d'enquêter sur les événements survenus en France de 1933 à 1945" was subsequently published over several years and includes a great deal of detailed testimony on tank issues.

ARTICLES

Avignon, Roger, "À la poursuite des Chars B inconnus", *Guerre, Blindés & Materiél*, No. 80, December 2007, pp. 24–31.

Avignon, Roger, "Les Chars B1 bis de la 2e DCR: I-Les premiers combats de 8e BCC 15–20 mai 1940", *Steelmasters*, No. 16, August 1996.

Avignon, Roger, "Les Chars B1 bis de la 2e DCR: II-Les premiers combats de 15e BCC 15–20 mai 1940", *Steelmasters*, No. 17, October 1996.

Avignon, Roger, "Les Chars B1 bis de la 3e DCR: La 5e Demi-brigade Lourde au combat 1940", *Steelmasters*, No. 6, December 1994.

Barbanson, Eric, "Les AMR Schneider P16 du 6ᵉ GRDI dans la bataille de Stonne", *Guerre, Blindés & Materiél*, No. 90, January 2010, pp. 26–33.

Bonnaud, Stéphane, "Au 49ᵉ BCC avec les Chars B", *Guerre, Blindés & Materiél*, No. 87, April 2009, pp. 36–57.

Bonnaud, Stéphane, "Le 49ᵉ BCC à Stonne", *Guerre, Blindés & Materiél*, No. 88, September 2009, pp. 40–57.

Dagnicourt, Eric, "Le 45ᵉ Bataillon de Chars de la Gendarmerie", *Guerre, Blindés & Materiél*, No. 82, April 2008, pp. 26–35.

Denis, Eric, "Le bataille de Stonne", *Batailles*, Thématique no. 2, 2008, pp. 4–81.

Gunsberg, Jeffery, "The Battle of Gembloux 14–15 May 1940: The Blitzkrieg Checked", *Journal of Military History*, No. 64, January 2000, pp. 97–140.

Rottgardt, Dirk, "Die deutsche Panzertruppe am 10.5.1940", *Zeitschrift für Heereskunde*, Nr. 319, May–June 1985, pp. 61–67.

Vauvillier, François, "De Gaulle, Reynaud, et le Corps spécialisé", *Guerre, Blindés & Materiél*, No. 85, October 2008, pp. 22–37.

Vauvillier, François, "La Division cuirassée en 1940 et ses perspectives", *Guerre, Blindés & Materiél*, No. 79, October 2007, pp. 38–49.

Vauvillier, François, "Mais ou sont donc passes nos Chars B ? ", *Guerre, Blindés & Materiél*, No. 77, June 2007, pp. 26–37.

Vauvillier, François, "Notre cavalerie méchanique à son apogée le 10 mai 1940", *Guerre, Blindés & Materiél*, No. 75, February 2007, pp. 40–49.

Vauvillier, François, "Produire le Char B : Défi ou chimère? ", *Guerre, Blindés & Materiél*, No. 76, April 2007, pp. 36–49.

BOOKS

Autant, Jean-Paul, *La bataille de Stonne mai 1940: Un choc frontal durant la campagne de France* (Bénévent: 2010)

Boly, René, *Fallait-il sauver le char Bayard? Le 41eme BCC Aubigny-sur-Nère, Ardennes, Champagne* (Association Ardennes: 2003)

Bonnaud, Stéphane, *Chars B au combat: Hommes et materials du 15e BCC* (Historie et Collections: 2002)

Citino, Robert, *Quest for Decisive Victory: From Stalemate to Blitzkrieg in Europe 1899–1940* (University Press of Kansas: 2002)

Clarke, Jeffrey, *Military Technology in Republican France: The Evolution of the French Armored Force 1917–40* (UMI: 1970)

Danjou, Pascal, *Char B1 bis* (Barbotin: 2009)

Danjou, Pascal, *Les Chars B: B1, B1 bis, B1 ter,* (Barbotin: 2005)

Doughty, Robert, *The Breaking Point: Sedan and the Fall of France 1940* (Archon: 1990)

Doughty, Robert, *The Seeds of Disaster: The Development of French Army Doctrine 1919–1939* (Archon: 1985)

Esser, Willi, *Dokumentation uber die Enteicklung und Erprobung der ersten Panzerkampfwagen der Reichswehr* (Krauss-Maffei: 1979)

Ferrard, Stephane, *France 1940: L'armement terrestre* (ETAI: 1998)

Fish, Kevin, *Panzer Regiment 8 in World War II: Poland-France-North Africa* (Schiffer: 2008)

Forty, Jonathan, *Tanks in detail: Panzer IV Ausf A to J* (Ian Allen: 2002)

Freiser, Karl-Heinz, *The Blitzkrieg Myth: The 1940 Campaign in the West* (Naval Institute Press: 2005)

Guderian, Heinz, *Panzer Leader* (Dutton: 1957).

Habeck, Mary, *Storm of Steel: The Development of Armor Doctrine in Germany and the Soviet Union 1919–1939* (Cornell University Press: 2003)

Horne, Alistair, *To Lose a Battle: France 1940* (Little, Brown: 1969)

Jeudy, Jean-Gabriel, *Chars de France* (ETAI: 1997)

Kiesling, Eugenia, *Arming against Hitler: France & the Limits of Military Planning,* (University Press of Kansas: 1996)

Mary, Jean-Yves, *Le Corridor des Panzers: Par-delà la Meuse 10–15 mai 1940* (Heimdal: 2010)

May, Ernest, *Strange Victory: Hitler's Conquest of France* (Hill and Wang: 2000)

Restayn, J. and Moller, N., *The 10.Panzer Division* (Federowicz: 2003)

Rothburst, Florian, *Guderian's XIX Panzer Corps and The Battle of France: Breakthrough in the Ardennes, May 1940* (Praeger: 1990)

Saint-Martin, Gérard, *L'arme blindée française, Tome 1: Mai–Juin 1940, Les blindés français dans la tourmente* (Economica: 1998)

Showalter, Dennis, *Hitler's Panzers: The Lightning Attacks that Revolutionized Warfare* (Berkley-Caliber: 2010)

Spielberger, Walter, *Panzer IV and its Variants* (Schiffer: 1993)

INDEX

References to illustrations are shown in **bold**.